TO HAIR AND BACK

My Journey Toward Self-Love
One Strand at a Time

A Memoir

Rhonda Eason

Published by Rhonda Eason

v2

ISBN-10:
0-9991188-0-3

ISBN-13:
978-0-9991188-0-1

Cover design by Rhonda Eason
Cover photo courtesy of 123RF

AUTHOR'S NOTE

This story is my own. I write of my personal experiences and do not assume that all women of color will have the same experiences, lessons, beliefs or takeaways. Therefore, I cannot and dare not, speak for anyone other than myself.

My memory is not what it used to be. I'm old. I admit it. However, I have taken great care to write truthfully of each of these experiences. Nevertheless, all names have been changed (except where noted) to protect the privacy of the innocent…and the guilty.

OTHER TITLES BY RHONDA EASON

Jaded

Sweet Secrets

Man for Hire
(a novella)

COMING SOON

Nobody's Angel

This book is dedicated to all my sisters who have finally
discovered the greatest love of all.
And also to those still searching.

Few people of any race wear completely natural hair.
If they did, we would be a nation of Unibombers.

Roger Ebert

1

Hair is the first thing. And teeth the second. Hair and teeth.

A man got those two things, he's got it all.

James Brown

Mrs. Fletcher

It was all Mrs. Fletcher's fault. I'd never seen anyone like her before. She was as dark as a blackberry, her skin smooth in its rich creaminess. She had prominent cheekbones and wore a muted berry color over her thick lips. Round spectacles complemented her modern-day schoolmarm vibe. Mrs. Fletcher's clothes were timeless classics. She'd pair a knee-length plaid skirt with a flowy white blouse that tied in a bow at her clavicle. Her boots were high-heeled (something my mother would never wear). But flawless skin, fashionable clothes, and her very essence paled in comparison to her hair. There she stood in front of a room filled with my peers—mostly lower-income inner city second-graders in Detroit— looking every bit the epitome of style and grace. She was my personal Jackie O.

But, oh.

My God.

Her hair.

Impossibly bone straight, Mrs. Fletcher's hair was something that I'd never seen on a black woman. It had the perfect trifecta. The holy grail I would chase my entire life: length, bounce, and straightness. Women who had that type of hair had men who wanted to be with them, women who wanted to be like them. They had happiness and love and beauty. I knew this mindset was true because I saw it reflected on TV and in magazines.

I was one of Mrs. Fletcher's favorites—for Christmas she once gave me a purse stuffed with candy. Of course I was one of her favorites. Who wouldn't adore a child who looked up at you—literally—mouth slightly parted (watering?), breathless, and dazed by the sight of your loveliness? Her hair—no, it was far too lush to be called something so generic—her bountiful tresses stopped just at her shoulders. She wore it curled under in the back, and from ear to ear around the front of her face, she wore a perfect flip. There was never a hair out of place. When she walked, it bounced. When she bent forward, her dark black locks followed freely like a trapeze artist flying through the air. I longed to run my fingers through her hair. I imagined it would feel like feathers. It would feel the exact opposite of my thick, tightly wound, impossible-to-comb kinks.

"Jesus had hair of wool," my mother told me one day while I cried as she wrangled with my hair. "Never forget that. John the Baptist said that Jesus had hair like wool. So you can feel good knowing that God blessed you with hair like His only begotten son."

Actually, it's written that his head and hair were *white* like wool, which means Jesus had a slightly different situation going on. But the distinction wouldn't have made a whit of difference to me. So what if his hair was thick like wool? I was neither flattered nor proud that my hair was a short kinky conundrum that flummoxed my mother—her of the silky straight Native-American-in-her-veins hair.

My mother, my two older half sisters, even my maternal grandmother, with whom we lived, all had hair textures very different from one another. Yet they all had manageable, dare I say, *good* hair. I was the black sheep with the hair to match. I was the only one in the family who had hair that could hold a pick without it falling out. My desire to be "normal" and to look like the other students grew with my deepening obsession with hair. The perfect hair would make a chubby, dark-skinned, nappy-headed little girl feel whole, feel beautiful. But not any kind of hair. Certainly not kinky hair. It had to be silky, straight hair.

No, wait. It had to be long, curly hair.

No, it had to be shoulder-length hair with waves.

Or curly hair that was really, really big.

Or...

Oh, hell. What kind of hair would make me happy? Satisfied to be in my own skin? What kind of hair would make me feel that I belonged? Feel whole? Feel pretty?

Mrs. Fletcher is to blame for showing me the heights black hair could achieve. Totally her fault.

Had I never seen a black woman up close with a mane like hers back there in 1980, that little seven-year old girl might not have set out on a lifelong journey to find the perfect hair.

Damn you, Mrs. Fletcher. And your friggin' fantastic head of hair.

2

We must accept finite disappointment, but never lose
infinite hope.

Martin Luther King, Jr.

Don't Bite the Hand That Braids You

We sat on the porch of our old neighborhood stuffing
ourselves on a hot summer day with pint-sized cartons of
ice cream. Rocky road for Ma. Mint chocolate chip for me.
The little square 99-cent cartons were a perfect way to kiss
summer good-bye. Although we had pretty much been
kissing summer good-bye almost every week since school
ended in late May with the creamy goodness. Now it was
August, and school would be grinding into gear soon.

I liked it when it was like this—just Ma and me. My oldest sister, Nina, sixteen, and seven years my senior, was around the corner at her boyfriend's house with her two-year-old son in tow. Toya, the fifteen-year-old Lolita of the family, was allegedly at her girlfriend's house. Yeah, okay. Besides being the stand-out beauty among us, she was also smart, with the trophies to prove it. But not smart enough for Ma to believe that girlfriend story. Ma was too busy working and going to school to watch us every second of the day. And as the old adage goes: teenagers with raging hormones will be teenagers with raging hormones.

Often, Ma would say some variation of, "Y'all mess around and get knocked up, you'd better have a place lined up to live."

Nina had proven that was an empty threat. Ma, trying to educate herself and pull us up out of poverty, fought an uphill battle with those two. While I, precocious and competitive, observed. I jockeyed to be her favorite by being good and following the rules. Hence, she and I together, just the two of us, soaking up the sun and eating ice cream, was my idea of time well spent.

On that particular day, Grandma was at a church event, doing what Ma and I probably should have been doing— socializing. But we were odd ducks. Even at that young age, I was aware of the fact that she and I didn't have personalities that drew people toward us. Our neighborhood on Dunedin Street bustled with summertime activity. One house blared Laura Branigan's "Gloria," while a car down the street battled with its own eight-track of Donna Summer's "Love is in Control."

"Rhonda, toss these cartons out, then go upstairs and get me a comb so I can get started on your hair."

What had I done to deserve that special hell? I turned to her, incredulous. "You're going to do my hair?"

"Yes, why does that sound so strange? School's coming up next week."

That was exactly the point. School was coming up, and I didn't want to return displaying my mother's clumsy attempt at hairstyling. I suspected I looked odd enough as it was. Nevertheless, I did as she bade.

When I returned to the porch with a comb and jar of Blue Magic grease, I settled between her plump thighs on the wooden slabs of the porch. Ma proceeded to work the kinks out of my hair with the thick plastic comb.

"I thought I was gonna get my hair braided by Ms. Lena," I whined. My mother was as adept at combing my hair as she was at building a house from the ground up. Not to mention she didn't know her own strength. You'd think she was tending a matted dog. Ouch!

"Yeah well..." her voice trailed off.

I cried out as a particularly tight kink tangled with the comb and pulled at my sensitive scalp.

"There's Mama coming," Ma said. If it was meant as a distraction, it didn't help. I wailed.

Moments later Grandma climbed the steps of the porch.

"Hey, there," she said, ever cheerful. Pieces of her gray curly wig peaked out from beneath her small, round church hat. She was dressed in her Sunday best even though it was Saturday. Grandma loved herself some church. "I brought back some leftovers for Mary. You think she home?"

Miss Mary lived in the bottom right apartment in our building. We lived in a four-family flat: our family occupied the top right apartment; our aunts occupied the top left. The owner of the place occupied the last apartment.

"Yeah, she's in there," Ma said. "She was out here not too long ago."

Grandma watched Ma's attempt at hair grooming for a few minutes, then said, "I thought Lena usually braid that child's hair. You ain't got the twenty dollars?"

"It ain't 'bout the twenty dollars, Momma. I got the money."

"Oh yeah?" Grandma eyed me doubtfully. She had this way of moving her bottom jaw from side to side. I think she was realigning her dentures or something. "Cause I got twenty dollars if you don't."

"Mama," Ma snapped, doing a poor job of wrangling in her rising temper. "I said I got the money. Can't I do my own child's hair?"

Grandma studied my pinched face that bordered on tears. Then she said in a quiet tone, "She usually pretty good about the braiding."

"She and I fell out," Ma said in a there-are-you-happy? tone.

"Sho nuff?" Grandma said, not at all surprised. This was not a new occurrence. Ma and people ... well, it was kinda like oil and water: both liquids ... but very different kinds that didn't mix well.

Ma dropped her hands to her knees, exasperated, and studied the thick bush on top of my head like it was clay waiting to be designed into art.

"She'd probably still braid Rhonda's hair," Ma mumbled.

Grandma removed her pink suit jacket. "It would be the Christian thing to do."

"You shouldn't bring a child into an adult's mess," Ma argued with herself.

"No, you shouldn't," Grandma concurred, although it sounded more like a question.

"And I know she could use the money."

"Annette, why don't you do like you always do and take her on down there with the money? I'm sure she won't mind braiding Rhonda's hair."

Moments later I was headed down the street to the last house on the corner with money in my hand, glad that Ms. Lena was going to do my hair. She could do all kinds of neat designs from cornrows in zigzags or a thousand individual braids with pretty beads on the ends that rattled when I shook my head. That cost a lot more money and took a lot of time. Sometimes she made me cry, too, when she combed my hair but with her I always knew the end result would be worth it.

Ms. Lena sat on the porch smoking a cigarette. Her girlfriends and a bunch of kids surrounded her.

"Lord, would you looka here," said one woman. I didn't know her, but it sure seemed like she knew me. They all stared at me like a martian had landed from Venus.

"She got some nerve," another woman I didn't know whispered loud enough for me to hear.

"Tamisha ain't here, baby," Ms. Lena said, even though she knew I wasn't there to see her daughter. My hair stood straight up to the sky, hinting at Ma's abandoned attempt at grooming. "She gone wit' her daddy."

I looked at the ladies on the porch. Ms. Lena's son, William, was five years old and playing with a plastic truck.

I said, "Ma sent me down here to get my hair braided." I held out the money that had been placed in my hand by Ma with a promise of an ass-whooping if I lost it.

"Lord," the women said in unison.

I was starting to get the impression that Ma had done something wrong and I was caught in the middle of it.

Ms. Lena, a woman who had braided my hair on multiple occasions, took a long drag of her cigarette.

"I'm sorry, little girl," she said, as if to a stranger, as if she hadn't braided my hair a gazillion times. Smoke billowed from her nose and mouth. "Tell ya mommy I can't braid ya hair no more."

What? I wanted to cry. I wanted Ms. Lena to braid my hair! What had Ma done? I loved when Ms. Lena gave me a zillion braids with beads that made beautiful music every time I turned my head. And I constantly turned my head.

But I was a kid. A kid mixed up in adult mess that I knew nothing about so I said, "Okay," and headed back down the street with unkempt hair.

Ma's face fell when she saw me walking home. She twisted her lips in disgust.

"I can't believe she would say no to a child. You ain't got nothing to do with what's going on between us."

"Well my Lord," Grandma said, appalled by the non-Christian behavior. "What happened, Annette?" She had changed out of her Sunday best into a flower-print housedress.

"It ain't nothing, Mama," she replied dismissively to Grandma. "I'll put your hair in a ponytail, and we'll call it a day."

My hair in a ponytail would mean a daily combing, which meant daily hollering from my tender-headed self. It would be painful for all involved, but mostly me. I seethed at Ma in silence. This was her fault. She'd gone and messed up a good thing with Ms. Lena. I didn't know what she did, but I knew she'd done something.

I hated the fact that Ma couldn't manage my hair herself. Didn't *every* mother know how to do her daughter's hair? Wasn't that why women wished they'd have a girl, so they could play with her hair? And Ms. Lena! How could she do this to me? We were at her mercy, and this was how she treated us?

There was nothing I could do about the situation. Grandma would sometimes say that we all have our cross to bear. My young mind learned early that my hair was my albert tross, or something like that.

3

All of us have ways in which we mask and cover our pain.
Iyanla Vanzant

The Shirt Phase

It was as if they had never seen a shirt before. My family stared at me as though I was an intriguing exhibition that had walked out of the Detroit Institute of Arts and had a seat at their table. Didn't they get it? No, from the looks they were giving me from around the table they most certainly did not get it. They were probably still of the antiquated belief that shirts were for wearing on the torso only.

I had stumbled upon my new hair quite by accident. It was a rule in our house that when you returned home from school, you removed your good clothes and put on your play clothes. Mind you, since we were living in a Detroit ghetto, the distinction between the two was a fine one. Anyway, there I was, always looking for a shortcut, when I decided to pull my button-down shirt up over my head instead of unbuttoning each button.

Then a miracle happened. My shirt got stuck on my head. I hadn't unbuttoned the top button, and I became tangled in my shirt; but somehow, I managed to get my arms through. Then I felt it. The weight of it. The swing of it. I closed my eyes, and I could see myself in my imagination: a beautiful black girl with lustrous long locks. I wrapped the arms of the shirt around the body of the garment. There. A ponytail. I looked in the mirror. The purplish plaid shirt wasn't quite as natural looking as I had envisioned. But gosh dang it, it had swing! And wasn't that what the good life was all about? Having hair that swung? Hair that fell over one's shoulders as a testament to one's ultra-femininity? Yes, long hair was where true beauty lived. And now that I had it—albeit via 100 percent polyester—this little beauty queen was ready for prime time.

"What the…?"

That from Toya. Annoying as ever. At fourteen, she was always so quick with the mouth.

"What is that on your head?" she asked.

I ignored her. What could she understand about my journey? She was blessed with a thick, long mane that curled up into perfect bushels of corkscrews with a touch of water and gel. When worn in a ponytail, Toya's hair—as yet untouched by relaxers—bore deep waves that cascaded across her crown and hung like corn silk down her back. She was the luckiest of the bunch of lucky women in our household. And she hated her natural hair. As big sisters go, they're all pretty much egotistical know-it-alls, but she really took the cake.

The six of us (including my baby nephew) sat at the table making small talk about news and entertainment and such. Toya, quieter than usual, was off in her own world. I imagined she was mentally spelling words in her head to prepare for the upcoming Regional Spelling Bee. Or she was thinking about boys. I imagined her thoughts were usually on one or the other.

At fourteen, Nina, our oldest sister, was most likely wondering when dinner would be over so she could sneak over to her boyfriend's house. Her teen pregnancy last year had caught the family by surprise—especially Ma, who constantly worked menial jobs à la the seamstress, cashier, housekeeper variety, while attending night school. Nina was a quiet girl who'd latched on to her boyfriend like a leech to a host. To say her relationship with Ma had turned tense would be an understatement. As for my thoughts on Nina's teen pregnancy, well! Babies having babies made a baby like me never want to have babies ever in life.

Nina looked at me, her mouth full of fried pork chop, and shook her head as if not even trying to figure out my new, sleek 'do. Her perfect mushroom haircut was a direct rip-off of Tootie from *Facts of Life*. She even had a similar grade of hair as Tootie so what could she know of my plight?

I was an alien among swans.

"Rhonda." My mother said my name as if all the life had been sucked out of her. As if *I* was the one sucking the life out of her. She looked tired. Dark circles formed beneath her eyes. Ma was up routinely, into the wee hours of the morning, studying. She attended a local college in hopes of getting a bachelor's degree in accounting. She was good with figuring out tough problems. When she was a teenager in Augusta, Georgia, back in the early sixties, my mother got sick of being embarrassed by her fall-down-drunk alcoholic father. She stayed up at night, plotting how to get out of his house. Finally, one night at a local club she figured out the answer. She got knocked up by and married the teenaged bass player performing in the band. With him, she had two girls—Nina and Toya. They'd created two girls with beautiful—albeit different—grades of hair. When Ma tired of Mr. Bass Player banging on her body like she was a drum set, her head started figuring again, calculating the odds of survival in his house and out of it. This time, she used her connections up north to find her next opportunity. Ma packed up her two girls and hightailed it out of Georgia and to New Jersey where she worked at McGuire Air Force Base. That's where she met a military man—my father. History repeated itself, and another romantic relationship soured. Not long after that, she migrated to Detroit with three kids in tow and crashed in on Grandma's good time living the single life. The five of us crammed into her two-bedroom flat, the landmark location where I debuted my polyester ponytail.

"Rhonda," Ma began again with exasperation, "why are you wearing a shirt on your head?"

"It's not a shirt," I explained calmly. "It's my hair."

Cackles arose from the peanut gallery formed by my sisters.

"It is not your hair," my mother explained—as if I didn't know. As if I was retarded. "It is your shirt. And I think it's your school shirt. If you mess up your school shirt, I am not buying you another one before the end of the school year."

"I'm not gonna mess it up."

"Annette," my grandmother said. "She shouldn't wear that mess at the dinner table. She shouldn't wear it at all."

"Rhonda, you shouldn't wear that at the dinner table," my mother repeated like a weary parrot.

"But it's my hair. Grandma don't have to take off her wig at the dinner table. Why do I have to take off my hair?"

"Don't you talk about Grandma like that!" Nina snapped, compulsively protective of Grandma.

"I wasn't talking about her. I'm just saying."

Toya contributed to the conversation with "What is wrong with her?"

"She wants to be white," Ma said and turned to me, "Honey, you've got to learn to love the skin God gave you."

There. It was said. It wasn't hinted at or scurried around. Those words were repeated. Often. Rhonda wants to be white. As if they didn't know who my idol was. As if I didn't talk about Mrs. Fletcher obsessively.

My mother said it, sure, but it was a collective thought, shared amongst my family. Undeterred, every day I came home from school and put on my hair. Different shirts and sweaters gave me a different look and feel. T-shirts made me feel as though I was headed to the beach while sweaters made me feel as though I was headed to a gala.

This phase of my life was before Whoopi Goldberg stepped onto the scene in an HBO standup comedy special where she included a routine about a young black girl who wore a similar garment on her head and pretended it was her hair. (I often wondered how she knew there was a black girl actually doing that in the world? Did that mean I wasn't the only one?) The difference between that character and me was that I never associated hair with skin color. I did not think I was white nor did I want to be. My family, however, didn't get that. They thought I was influenced by television commercials and magazines that promoted white beauty. And maybe to an extent I was. I could hardly wait to get the latest edition of the Sears Catalog delivered to our door so I could stare at Iman with equal ardor as I stared at Cheryl Tiegs.

But all I wanted was the hair. And I wanted *all* of the hair—no one particular look or type. Diana Ross, Tina Turner, Beverly Johnson, Christie Brinkley, Brooke

Shields, Farrah Fawcett. I wanted to scalp them all and place their tendrils on my peanut-shaped head.

Still, my family's general impression of me was that I was a confused little black girl who wanted to be a little white girl. Talk about misguided. It would be years before I understood how damaging it was for my family to assign that belief system to me without my participation. The natural process of growing up makes a female challenge and form a core belief system about herself. Who needs the added input from confused, opinionated bystanders?

It would be years until I stopped trying to prove my blackness to my family. I wanted to be me. I wanted to be the best version of me. And I would be, as soon as I could rid myself of the thicket of matted corkscrews on my head and wear upon my crown the absolute perfect head of hair.

4

Everything has beauty, but not everyone sees it.

Confucius

The Perm

Ma was a study in contradictions. As a child I knew my mother to be a hardworking student. While working a multitude of low-wage jobs and raising three kids as a single parent, Ma managed to get her GED. Apparently, she'd figured out that a high school dropout from Georgia with no discernible talents wasn't destined to get very far in the world. After she earned her GED, she set her sights on a loftier goal: an associate's degree in accounting. I remember getting home from elementary school, only one block from our house on Linwood, and my mother rushing me to put some food in my belly and do my homework so we could hit the road. We'd take a city bus on the thirty-minute ride destined for Dearborn Community College. Ma planted me in the school cafeteria (practically empty at five or six in the evening) where she left me with pocket change for the vending machines and a stern warning: "You do not come to my class unless it's an emergency, you got that? Stay here and don't move."

I moved. I always moved. To her, however, I nodded my headed in tacit understanding. But I got bored. And I was anxious to be an adult and attend college. I'd roam around the halls of the small school as though I was a student headed toward a class. I'd find Ma's classroom and, on more than one occasion, poke my head inside to see if she really was where she said she'd be. In return, I got that silent cold glare from her that black women are so known for giving. *Embarrass me*, her eyes said, *and I will beat your ass when we get home.* My mischievous eyes smiled back at her as though saying, *Maybe. But you can't whoop me around all these good white folks. Ha, ha!* I said nothing. I slumped to the floor and listened to the professor, happy for even this remote nearness to my mother.

Ma had a thing about being embarrassed. It's one of the intangible gifts that she passed on to me. Parents do that, don't they? They pass down their insecurities and fears to their kids as if to say, *Here, don't say I never gave you anything. Maybe you'll have better luck with it than I did.* I think Ma's fear of embarrassment was a throwback to her days of living in Georgia in the fifties. She didn't like to bring attention to herself. My mother was a four-foot-eleven plump woman with dark skin and average face. She was quick to call herself ugly, but I never thought so. Even with the scar above her right eye from a long-ago car accident, I thought my mother was a vision of loveliness with her perfect row of teeth and round cheeks and warm, super-soft hugs.

Eventually, I would tire of the professor, and I'd make my way back down to the cafeteria for a soda or candy. I completed whatever homework I didn't have time to finish at home or on the bus. Then I read one of my many library books like *Encyclopedia Brown* by Donald J. Sobol or anything by Beverly Cleary or Judy Blume. Reading was my companion because I had few real friends. I could relate to characters better than people, and the books kept me entertained for hours on end. It would be another twenty years before I picked up a book with characters who actually looked like me, complete with brown skin and unmanageable hair. Bebe Moore Campbell, Alice Walker, and Terry McMillan weren't writing children's books. And if there were writers who wrote stories about black girls solving mysteries, thwarting bullies, or simply experiencing the deliciousness of first love, that fact would have been as incomprehensible to me as if you'd told me that one day I'd watch television shows on my telephone. It wouldn't have made sense. Watching *Good Times* from a rotary phone? Get out of here.

Just as my mother dedicated herself to her education, to pulling her family out of poverty, to making a contribution to society, she equally resisted other tasks that she found less rewarding. For example, Ma never cleaned the house.

"I've got three kids," she'd argue. "Why would I clean the house? That's what you're for."

And her sense of nutrition and health were skewed.

"I haven't had a drop of alcohol in almost twenty years. And haven't smoked a cigarette in ten," she boasted on one of the rare occasions when she and all of her girls were in the same room. (She'd later pick up smoking again.) "And never did drugs a day in my life. Not even marijuana. No sir. Don't need nothing playing with my mind."

"Ma, can I have some of your Halloween candy?" I asked one fall day.

"You can have the candy corn."

"I want the peanut butter candy, with the soft center."

"I bought each of you a two-pound big bag of peanut butter candy so you wouldn't need any of mine. So no."

"Please," I whined. "I ate all mine."

"I said no. There's ice cream in the fridge, go get some of that."

Just say no to drugs. Just say yes to sugar. Lots and lots of sugar. We were a house full of sugar-addicted females.

"And bring me that perm kit while you're at it," she said in a tone that suggested she'd done the crime of buying it, she might as well do the time and put it on my hair. "Might as well get this over with."

Combing my hair was on par with vacuuming: laborious, ear-piercing, and time-consuming. And the next day, she'd examine her finished product and realize it looked only marginally better than before she'd started.

I sat at the kitchen table while my mother's squinted eyes studied the typewritten instructions on the perm kit. We called it a perm back then, but technically, it was a relaxer because it straightened the natural curls of our hair.

"Hmm ... instructions say for coarse hair I should keep on no longer than twelve minutes. I'm gonna let it sit longer to make sure we get your hair good and straight. They don't make these home kits all that strong. What's the worst that can happen?"

I envisioned myself going to school the next day with all my kinks straightened. My hair would probably go all the way to my neck! I'd be able to swing it, and it'd flip and flop and blow as I walked.

"Ouch!" I yelled.

"Be still and let me comb it out first."

My hair was an odd display. Small peas or naps or kinks (pick your adjective) trailed across the front of my head from ear to ear. The kitchen (or nape) was the two-inch section of hair that extended from the base of my neck up to the midpoint of my ears, just below the crown. My hair simply refused to grow back there. The rest of my hair was most often pulled up into a singular ponytail. That ponytail—short, dry, and stiff as a twig—was a three-inch twist that stuck up toward the sky at a 45-degree angle, like a television antenna. Alfalfa's hair from *The Little Rascals* was a creative, humorous godsend. My hair was a vengeful one.

Ma held my head firmly with one hand as the comb tugged at the hair at my nape. My tender scalp screamed out in pain.

"Your kitchen is the worst part of your head."

Tears streamed from my eyes as the teeth of the plastic comb wrestled with the thick, matted carpet of my hair.

Ma said, "Lord Jesus help me."

He didn't. The comb broke.

Ma's temper began to rise. My demonstrative protestations wore on her nerves.

"All right, that's enough! Let's get this over with."

My mother put on the plastic gloves included in the kit, then mixed the chemicals. "Now it's going to burn after awhile, Rhonda. I want you to stand it as long as possible so your hair can get straight."

"Okay," I agreed through sobs. If a little burning was all it took to look like Pamela Grier then burn, baby burn!

Dear. God. It stung.

Ma smoothed the acrid-smelling chemicals through my hair. She was an untrained hairstylist who hadn't a clue beyond the printed instructions as to what she was doing. And she didn't even realize she wasn't following the instructions carefully. Ma ran the comb through the entire length of my hair to smooth the kinks, not just the new growth. She pressed down hard until I could feel the tingling cream against my scalp. It felt as though my scalp was being burned apart and detaching from my skull. The slow burn spread across my head. I bit my lip. Ma continued on her mission to make her youngest child look presentable in school, to make her hairdressing duties manageable at home.

The timer buzzed when we'd reached the recommended maximum time—twelve minutes.

"Can you stand it a little longer?"

I couldn't, but I nodded.

Ma kept smoothing. And smoothing. And smoothing.

"I promise you, one day you're gonna be so happy to have thick, coarse hair like this. It's really the best kind."

Even I knew she was trying to make the ugly duckling of the family feel less so. It wasn't working.

I clinched my legs, squeezed my eyes.

"I'm ready, I'm ready." I squirmed in my seat after what felt like an hour.

"Okay. I'll rinse it out," Ma said, her voice full of hope. The irritation she'd displayed moments ago already a memory. "We kept it in there way past the max time, and you did fine. They include those times so fools don't get too carried away, but you can always leave it in there a little longer. Come on, lean down in the tub."

I leaned my head down beneath the tub's faucet, a towel pressed tight against my eyes to prevent blindness. Ma hummed a tune while the cool water whisked away the creamy sodium hydroxide from my hair. Another name for sodium hydroxide is lye. It's a caustic acid that burns through skin. It's so thorough in it's ability to burn that a man working with a Mexican drug cartel once admitted to using the substance to dispose of three hundred bodies.

My scalp was on fire. I danced in my seat as much from the anticipation of my new silky strands as from the third degree burns that were forming on my tender scalp. The burning was made worse by the warm water touching it, like alcohol on an open wound.

"I told you not to scratch your head the day before a relaxer," Ma reminded me when I told her about a particularly burning section.

Oh, well. All girls knew that beauty was pain. We learned it as children, and our entire lives became a testament to this truth.

"Hmph," said Ma with curiosity. It was a singular word thick with wonderment and something else I couldn't quite distinguish. Concern? Confusion? It was the grunt you'd imagine coming from a person who stood in an empty lot where they'd parked their car moments ago, only to find the space empty.

I opened my eyes and stared at the ceiling while Ma rinsed the chemical from my head. She massaged in the neutralizing shampoo, agitating the skin even more. The woman did not know the strength of her hands.

"A little bit of hair broke off," she said, "but it's straight, that's for sure."

All I heard was 'it's straight.' That was good enough for me.

Ma hurriedly rinsed the soap from my head, applied the leave-in condition, and then used a blow dryer to get my strands super straight. The heat from the dryer tortured my irritated scalp further. Like whisking a lit match over already burned skin.

No expert with the curling iron, Ma gave me a few limp curls and then stood back and praised herself. "Not bad, Annette. Not bad at all."

I looked in the mirror and was pleased. My hair, short but silky, was finally as beautiful as I deserved. Ma didn't curl it too good, and some pieces were flipped in all kinds of weird directions. Never mind that. My naps were now straight. If I swung my head, my hair would follow.

I begged Ma to let me wear my hair down when I went to school the next day. My mother had been adamant that little girls should only wear ponytails and braids. This, however, was indeed a special occasion. I would finally look like a normal little girl with baby fine hair.

I would finally be beautiful.

5

All children are born pure egoists. They perceive their
needs to the exclusion of all others. Only through
socialization do they learn that some forms of gratification
must be deferred and others denied.

Andrew Vachss

Electrifying

The perm damaged my hair. It was gradual at first. The full
extent of the damage became clearer over the next few
weeks as the relaxer wore off and my hair reverted back to
the texture God gave me. (Perms—or relaxers—only last

about eight weeks and then have to be reapplied to the new growth.) Each day brought more hair shedding than the last. At first little bits of hair would fall to my shoulders, like the mild tremor of the earth before an earthquake. Then, as the wide-tooth comb slid with ease through my thinned hair, entire strands would break at the root and fall off, floating past my unamused eyes and landing on the sink. My kitchen got the worst of it. A huge swatch of hair broke off at my nape, leaving me near bald in the back. (The phenomenon of my hair breaking off at my nape up to my earlobe would afflict me well into adulthood. We'd suspected at the time that the friction between my coarse hair and my wool coat had caused the damage, and while that may have been a contributor, the hair loss continued even when I wore silk scarves to protect sensitive strands.)

The realization was as clear as the damaged dull black strands of hair in the ceramic bowl: My mother knew mothering, but tending hair and tending child were two completely separate entities. Ma had left the perm in for far too long and over the course of time, I was right back to feeling like a freak, albeit with mildly straight hair.

"Single-file line, Robert," our teacher reminded us as we walked down the hall toward the cafeteria. "Takisha, don't make me ask again."

I was already in line and ready to go. I was a foodie even then. No matter that my family was impoverished. We often ran out of food toward the end of the month, satisfying ourselves with sugar sandwiches or my personal favorite—Campbell's Cream of Mushroom Soup made with store brand milk when we had it to spare (and with water when we didn't).

I moved down the line and collected my milk and mystery meat hiding beneath a thick breading and sauce. Breakfast at school was better than lunch. We were in a program that gave kids from low-income homes free breakfast at school. I ate *real* cereal. The cereal brands that aired commercials during cartoons. Lunch was another matter. But it was still free food, and since I was not much into discriminating, I ate my mystery meat (legend has it that it wasn't a mystery—it was horse) and savored every bite.

When I was done eating, I lingered at the lunch table. The cause had nothing to do with the food.

"Hurry up, Rhonda," my teacher called. "Half the kids are already outside at recess. Hurry. You can't stay in here."

I didn't want to play. I didn't like how the kids liked to play. I didn't like how the *boys* liked to play. I'd lingered as long as I could, but eventually I had to get outside in the warm sunshine. I had to play. And be played with.

Maybe today would be different, I thought as I dragged my gym shoes across the peeling linoleum floor. Maybe today I'd be able to join a few of the girls jumping rope. That happened on occasion. Or maybe I'd climb the monkey bars. The key was not to run. Do. Not. Run.

"Hey, Rhonda. What you doing?"

"Nothing. Go on and leave me alone, Ricky."

Ricky was a beautiful boy. Cafe au lait skin, hazel eyes, and a bad-boy demeanor even though he wasn't old enough to have grown a hair anywhere except his head. From afar, an astute observer could look at a kid and identify the bully, the bullied, the class clown, and the popular, simply by the way they carried themselves. I, with the knotted roots and awkward personality, must have worn *bully me* in neon lights on my forehead. Ricky, by contrast, was a wiry boy with lean muscles starting to form and an attitude of uncultivated machismo. He was funny and cool which made him the perfect model of a bad boy. My feelings toward him were complicated. I liked him for being a cute boy who gave me more attention than I felt I deserved. And I hated him for the kind of attention he gave me.

Do. Not. Run.

"Let's go out onto the field," he suggested, his crew of boys behind him.

"No. I want to be by myself," I said, my back hugging the red brick wall behind me.

"What, you don't like playing with us?" he asked. "You think you better than us 'cause you talk proper?"

"No," I mumbled, my answer appropriate for either question.

Ricky was persistent, aggressive, the opposite of his cousin Gregory, on whom I also had a crush. We were all in the same fourth grade class, and if my feelings toward Ricky were complicated (at home I'd substitute his name in a popular song, singing in the mirror: *Hey, Ricky, you so fine, you so fine, you blow my mind, Hey Ricky. Hey, hey, hey Ricky!*) then my feelings toward Gregory were as pure and clear as a teardrop. He with the gentle personality, light eyes, curly brown hair. But it wasn't Gregory who was here now taunting me. It was Ricky.

"C'mon, Rhonda. Let me get a buzz," he said while his friends gathered around me, mischievous grins on their dirty little faces. The playground was busy with raucous kids running and laughing and screaming in merriment all around. The teachers couldn't be everywhere. They couldn't see everything.

"C'mon, Rhonda. I need to get electrified."

I began to walk away from them. Ricky came up behind me, put his fingers near my kitchen which was back to being kinky and curled low.

"Buzzzz," Ricky said and pretended to be electrocuted by my hair. His friends fell out in laughter.

Do. Not. Run.

"Stop," I said. I masked my growing anxiety with a half-grin on my face as though I thought being the butt of their joke was actually pretty funny. As if I was delighted that my kinky hair could bring amusement to their dull lives. I knew they wanted more than to play with my hair.

My adrenaline began to race. My heart thumped.

"It's electrifying!" Ricky said, reminiscent of John Travolta's character in *Grease*.

One by one, as I walked aimlessly through the playground, the boys took turns putting their fingertips to the nape of my neck, feigning electrical shock from my coarse hair, their entire bodies going limp from the imaginary jolt.

I couldn't bare it any longer. I shouldn't run. I knew that. But I couldn't not run. How could I stand there and let them mock me?

I couldn't outrun them. I knew that because I never had before. I also knew they were like dogs—the second you ran, they'd follow in hot pursuit—even if they didn't know what in hell they were running for.

But they knew....

I swatted a random hand away once more.

And then like a racehorse who hears the sound of a starter gun, fear got the best of me, and I was off.

My daily lunch time ritual had begun. I ran far from the school building—still on school grounds, my legs moving as fast and as far as they could take me out onto the field of grass. Ricky, the ringleader, caught up to me in no time and tackled me with all the focused effort of a college quarterback hoping to go pro. He covered me with his body. And then he pumped me. Hard.

Pumping. That's what we called it back then. Today, we'd call it dry humping. The legal system would call it sexual assault. At ten, our minds were more literal and less sexual. In fact, my entire youthful life I'd prove to be a slow learner when it came to sex. At that age, I vaguely knew sex existed, like one knew that divorce was a real thing somewhere in the world, but you couldn't really grasp the concept until it happened in your home.

On the field, far from the school building, Ricky's hips banged into mine over and over again. Sometimes, I fell forward, my face pressed into the ground. Other times I was on my back. It was a near-death experience each time, made more horrific by the fact that the other boys joined in. One by one? No, that would have been better—if this experience could be termed better. Instead, when Ricky fell onto me, his squad piled onto him. I always wondered if it ever occurred to them that only one of them was actually pumping a girl. The rest of them were pumping each other.

The experience was like having a four-hundred-pound pillow pressed on my seventy pound body, pushing down on my lungs, obstructing my nose, my mouth. Sometimes they pressed my head and neck into the grass, nearly smothering me. It was natural to lose my breath. Often times I lost my vision. When they were done, they'd get up, high fives all around, congratulating themselves for a job well done, then head off to other boyish adventures. Tomorrow would be another electrifying day.

6

You can be the moon and still be jealous of the stars.

Gary Allan

The Other Asset

"Barbiturates," Alicia Jones said crisply, as she sat on my front porch with me. My family lived in a mint green two-story house on Linwood Street on the west side of Detroit. It was conveniently located a block from my current school, Woodward Elementary, three houses down from Holy Cross Baptist Church, and a block away from my future middle school—McMichael.

"Marilyn Monroe committed suicide by taking too many barbiturates. Do you know what they are?"

I was honored to have Alicia Jones at my house, even if she was casting her intelligent eyes on me with unmasked condescension. She was a pretty girl with smooth skin the color of light brown sugar. Alicia wore her hair down, and in the warm breeze, it blew as though a gentle breath was constantly upon her. I wished I could know what it was like to be her, to awaken each day, slide a comb through her perfect hair without a tearful moment or broken plastic. What was it like to know that no one in school was going to pick on you because you were an above-average looking girl?

This was my chance to bond with a popular girl. To finally fit and bask in the glow of her short attention span. Alicia was a girl who came from a two-parent home (an anomaly in our lower-class neighborhood), a girl who went to the beauty salon (*the beauty salon!*) to get her hair pressed and curled. Those facts alone made her better than me. But to add the fact that her father was a pastor and her mother was a nurse only solidified in my mind that she was a princess and I was a pauper who should feel grateful to have her on my front stoop.

"No, I don't know what that is," I replied. I read books voraciously, and still I had not learned all the words in the world.

"They're depressants," she said, focusing on pulling the petals off a dandelion. "They make you feel relaxed and good. My dad taught me that word." She turned to me. "Where's your father?"

I swallowed hard. "Pittsburgh. He's a newspaper reporter."

"Oh. Why isn't he here with your momma?"

"They didn't get along."

That was an assumption on my part. After all, my father was out there. We were right here. One would think someone as smart as Alicia Jones could have made the same conclusion. I didn't want to talk about my father. Or my home. It would dim in comparison to hers. And I definitely didn't want her going inside. Our house was neat—my compulsive sisters made sure of that. They were the weirdo types who cleaned because they enjoyed it. But even they couldn't kill every roach that decided to wander from out of the walls and onto the living room table and sofas. What if one crawled onto Alicia? I already had enough to deal with at school. I couldn't be teased about my hair *and* our roaches.

"So…" Alicia said, "who do you like at school?"

I was grateful she let the family talk die. "Nobody."

"You've got to like someone," she said in perfect diction, more perfect than my own.

"I don't like anyone," I replied, mimicking her proper tone. "I think Gregory is kind of cute."

"Gregory McClintock? Yeah, he's cute. I heard Ricky likes you."

"Eww. I don't like Ricky."

"You do," she said, rolling her eyes. "You always let him run after you, and you let him get on top of you all the time."

"I don't let him do that."

"You haven't told on him."

No, I had not. If I had, I'd still have to be on the same playground with him. If he had practically suffocated me in good times, what would he do if I got him in trouble? And what would my mother think of me? She already thought I was a sexual deviant.

Once, in church, the pastor urged us all to pray, even if that meant we had to go in a closet for privacy. One day I went into the coat closet and shut the door, closed my eyes, and began to pray. Not long into my prayer, the closet door swung open, the light casting me in shame that I didn't understand.

"What are you doing in here?" my mother asked me. Her brown eyes scanned my body with open suspicion as I huddled on the floor under coats and between the vacuum cleaner and mop bucket.

"Nothing," I said. What kind of sinner would she take me for if I confessed what I was really doing? She'd swear I was lying. What could a kid possibly have to pray about?

"Um hmm, I bet you're not," she sneered. "Get out of the closet, and don't you ever let me catch you in there again!"

I crawled out of the small space, guilt over my uncommitted sin pushing me and my tears along. Anger at the pastor for setting me up to fail. Embarrassed for wanting to pray in the first place.

No, I did not confess to my mother about Ricky.

"See," Alicia said in a gotcha tone. "You like him. You know why all the boys like you, right?"

I knew. I didn't need her to tell me. I swallowed hard and watched the cars go by.

"They like you because you've got a big old butt!" Alicia laughed. "You've got the biggest butt in the whole class. The whole school even. I wouldn't want to walk around with that thing all the time."

"I don't mind."

"Anyway," she sighed, her humiliation of me complete. "I'd better get home."

Alicia let herself out of the gate and walked toward her own home on Wreford Street to the prettiest house on the block.

Why had she come by? She never came by to visit. Maybe it was to remind me not to get ahead of myself. To remind me that I wasn't getting masculine attention because of any special beauty. It was because I had a physical attribute the boys liked to play with. A derrière of epic proportion. In years to come, big butts would become en vogue. So much so that some women died from illegal butt injections. As a child, the idea of someone altering their bodies to get what I'd gotten naturally, of someone wanting something that caused me unwanted attention and shame, would have been as improbable as owning a television with three-hundred channels.

I watched Alicia jog across the street, her hair flopping on her head. She'd go home to her nice house and eat a balanced meal with her complete family while I played in the mirror with a shirt over my head, pretending I was her.

You didn't need to be an adult to realize how epically unfair life really was.

7

Children are very cruel, yes. Of course. Children are
extraordinarily cruel little creatures.

Dennis Potter

The Music Teacher

Everybody knew that Mrs. Carlisle did not play with
children. She taught children, yes. But she did not *play* with
them. Mrs. Carlisle ran her music class with the same
precision a drill sergeant ran a squad of wet-behind-the ears
recruits. She did not tolerate insolence. And lest we forget,
there was a five-inch long, one-inch thick piece of wood to
remind us. She was not a baby doll. She would not be toyed
with.

Although Mrs. Carlisle had the disposition of a stodgy old grandmother, she was actually quite young. Her smooth dark brown skin hadn't a line or wrinkle. She was a thin woman of average height with an angelic singing voice and a determination to help us grade- schoolers understand tone and pitch, and develop a deeper appreciation of music, if not develop our own musicality.

But we were elementary kids. We liked what we heard on the radio and weren't much interested in understanding how it all came together. Maybe boredom was to blame for what happened that day. It is said that idle hands are the devil's workshop. The rambunctious kids in class on that particular day were stirred with defiance in their veins. On that day, they weren't intimidated by Mrs. Carlisle or her notorious paddle.

There we sat in class on a day like any other. Three rows of about eight seats alongside the length of the wall. There was something different about Mrs. Carlisle on that day. Her hair. Her usual curly hair was tucked beneath a similar looking wig—a perfectly nice, unassuming wig—but a wig nonetheless. The length was short, the style conservative. There was also something else different about her that day. It was hard for a young kid to decipher, except that her aura was changed. She busied herself behind her desk with less assurance than normal. If she was coming into class with the hope that being surrounded by a bunch of loving, warm-hearted, innocent sixth graders would cure her of whatever seemed to be troubling her, she was wrong.

I heard it in the back row. The low murmur of whispers. Mrs. Carlisle heard it too and lifted her head from her desk. Usually the ice queen stare was enough to make us mind our manners. Not this time.

Giggles now. I turned my head to see who was the cause of the commotion. I hadn't the nerve to be so disruptive. Not to mention the paddle was an effective enough deterrent for me.

"Quiet," warned Mrs. Carlisle. "I am going to take roll and then start class. Until then, I want quiet."

I liked Mrs. Carlisle's wig. I understood wanting to wake up and look like someone else for a day. To let the dreams in your head become a reality. What I didn't quite understand was getting a wig that was so close to one's own hairstyle—almost as if trying to trick people into thinking it was her natural hair. My thinking was, if you were gonna put on a wig, then put on a *wig!* Go big, go wild, or go home. Nevertheless, I had a newfound feeling of kinship toward her. Even if I was deathly afraid of her and the wood she wielded.

While Mrs. Carlisle fiddled with her papers, the boys became restless, emboldened. Their whispers took on a fevered pitch. And then I heard it.

"Wiggy, wiggy, wiggy, wiggy!"

My stomach sunk in the way it does when one feels embarrassment on behalf of another.

The boys snickered.

Mrs. Carlisle looked up, her eyes searching for the miscreant. Was it possible that she knew the song? Of course she did. Even teachers couldn't resist the radio or avoid the quickly growing popularity of rap music.

The music group was called Newcleus. The song— "Jam on It"—could be heard blaring from a bedroom window or from a teenager's boom box while hanging out on the corner on any given afternoon. The song had nothing to do with hair. Yet, part of the chorus was a playfully childish robotic voice singing "wiggy, wiggy, wiggy, wiggy."

From the look on her face, the connection was not lost on Mrs. Carlisle.

"Who said that?" she asked.

The boys giggled amongst themselves. None of them was bold enough to fess up to singing, nor point fingers at the culprit.

"One more time," Mrs. Carlisle said and raised the thick piece of wood, "and I'm going to start handing out three licks."

There was something odd about Mrs. Carlisle's threat. While the words were clear and the threat—we knew—real, a hollowness echoed through her words. She chewed the inside of her lip while a pencil slipped from between her quivering fingers and landed on the floor. This delighted the boys. Mrs. Carlisle bent down to pick up the pencil.

"Wiggy, wiggy, wiggy, wiggy!"

This time it wasn't one boy. It was a gaggle of them. They sang in unison. They laughed aloud, delighted with their own mischief.

"Ricky! Get over here."

The smile disappeared from Ricky's face. He dragged himself up to the front of the class. Mrs. Carlisle picked up the paddle.

"Give me you hand."

Ricky held his palm out to her.

She rapped his hand with the paddle.

Whack!

Ricky squealed with each swat of the paddle.

Whack!

Whack!

Ricky sniffed, holding back his anger. He slogged back to his seat. His friends elbowed him. Ricky forgot about the pain despite the fact that tears welled in his eyes. He snickered. Again, the boys chanted, "Wiggy, wiggy, wiggy, wiggy!"

And again.

And again, they chanted.

It was like a dare. *You can't swat all of us, Mrs. Carlisle.*

Although I wasn't sure that was entirely true. Those of us in the first two rows craned our heads toward the back of the class, then to Mrs. Carlisle, and then back again.

What would happen now?

What happened was totally unexpected. Mrs. Carlisle whimpered. It was a mournful, painful sound. Her hand flew to her mouth. Tears blemished her face. She shook her head as if the last few minutes in class could be erased if she shook hard enough. As if the boys were part of a nightmare and all she had to do was clear her head, open her eyes, and they'd be gone.

Mrs. Carlisle, emotionally crippled by something that was beyond our understanding and crushed beneath the weight of the bullying, ran out of the classroom, shamed.

8

Never pick a fight with an ugly person, they've got nothing
to lose.
Robin Williams

My Mama Said

Being the youngest child in a house with two older siblings
didn't leave me much room for female bonding. On the
weekends, Nina my oldest sister, hung out with her son's
father, Tony, plotting their futures together. Toya, the
intellectual among us, was all breasts and hips by the time
she was twelve. Black Barbie with a brain. In the summer,
she trotted outside with her long, wavy hair flowing down
her back, her shoulders—the color of nutmeg—bare in a
summery top that strained to contain all of her.

And then there was me.

Too young for romantic entanglements and too introverted for female friendships, I had to find a way to entertain myself. Learn how to love your own company, Ma would say, as if she could see the future and knew this advice would help me cope with the inevitable loneliness that awaited me. If you don't like being with yourself, why should anybody else? You come in this world alone, and you leave this world alone. Learn how to live alone. Yada, yada, yada.

I suspect these words had fortified her against loneliness. People can only give you what they know.

"Rhonda, why don't you go outside and play?" my mother said irritably one day, cutting her narrow eyes at me.

Obviously, it wasn't a suggestion; it was an order. There were times when, despite the stress of being a single mother on welfare, struggling each day to pull herself up by her second-hand bootstraps, my mother was filled with the spirit of the Lord, mixed with a dab of sunshine and sugar. Then, there were moments like this. Without warning, a dark cloud passed overhead, her disposition turned sour. Ma's mood meter seemed to have three dials: infectious girlish delight, inexplicable mild irritation, and red hot anger.

I'd better hit the pavement while I was still in the mild irritation zone. I went outside into the summer heat and contemplated what to do. I hadn't fallen head over heels in love with books yet. That would come later, when I drifted into a habit that I unconsciously thought would unite me to my mother, because she was an avid reader, and my father, because he was a writer.

"They moving in," a voice from behind me said.

It was Leela, my best friend from the house across the empty lot. Best friend is a loose term. At that age, pretty much anybody your age who lives nearby qualifies as a best friend.

"I see that," I said as we both looked up the street at the moving truck that unloaded as many people as pieces of furniture.

"That's a big ol' family," Leela said. "I see a girl over there. You see her?"

I saw a lot of girls. There were four of them. And three boys. They even had two parents over there. Leela and I stood like spectators at a zoo watching this new sort of primate live their lives.

"It's so hot out here. Let's see if we can bake a mud pie!" Leela suggested.

I followed as she scrambled into our big backyard. There we sat, mixing ingredients of water, dirt, and grass until it formed the perfect consistency for a pie that surely wouldn't taste as delicious as it looked. And, of course, we bantered.

"My mama said," Leela began, "that it's a shame that yo mama let you walk around with your head looking like that."

What I felt was worse than a punch in the stomach. It was like watching someone punch my mother in the stomach and there was nothing I could do about it.

"My mama said that yo mama should be taking better care of you. Yo sisters' hair look fine but ... why can't yo mama do anything to yo head?"

"There's nothing wrong with my head," I responded meekly.

Okay, fine. The beads that aligned my head were short, dry, and nearly impossible to comb. My solitary two-inch ponytail was a static beacon that pointed to the sky. My hair wasn't pretty, I knew that, but worse than knowing that I had an unattractive head of hair was learning that other people knew it, too. People—strangers—saw me. And what they saw wasn't pretty. People in the neighborhood talked about me, in their homes, behind closed doors. How many people out there were talking about my mother and me? Leela's mother had slighted Ma and felt pity for me. Leela's mother looked at me as a victim of neglect, which was ridiculous. Didn't they know that my mother was awesome?

I already knew what my mother would say if I told her this. Her rants to us were legendary. *I don't care if someone calls me a bitch or any other name. They don't know me. Let them call me whatever they want. You don't have to defend my honor to strangers. Don't y'all ever get in a fight because someone calls me a name.*

If Ma said that fighting for her honor was stupid, then it probably was. But I was a kid who hadn't yet mastered the art of peace talks or turning the other cheek. So I balled up my fist and punched Leela in the face. We tussled in the backyard until she was tired of being pummeled. I may have had an unkempt head, but I had a mean headlock. She eventually ran home after I showed her mercy. As was our nature, we didn't speak to each other for a week. Then we were best friends again.

But I never forgot what her mother said about us.

9

You know how advice is. You only want it if it agrees with
what you wanted to do anyway.

John Steinbeck

The Warwicks

If I had been asked as an eight-year-old child, if my life up
until then was idyllic, I would have said yes. What did I
know of the poverty in which we lived? What did I know of
my mother's mental and emotional struggles? What I knew
for certain was that I had a doting grandmother, a hardworking mother, and two older sisters, all of whom kept me
safe. Afar, I had my father in Pittsburgh who called me
regularly, sent me presents (My heart still sings at the sight

of that big brown delivery truck!), and with whom I visited during summer vacations.

Our small apartment in the four-family flat was oftentimes filled with loud music, raucous laughter, and burgeoning hope that made the daily struggle of living tolerable. As far as my young eyes could see, we were as happy as a family could be. Up until then, I didn't know what fear meant. The closest association I'd had with the word was through watching scary movies that I'd been forbidden to watch. Scary, to me, was *The Elephant Man*. Ma told me the movie was not for kids, but I was adamant. I could handle it. I wanted to sit next to her on the ratty, plaid sofa and watch the movie. Ma, in her tough love sort of way, did not yell at me nor force me to leave. *You want to stay? Fine. You've got this coming....*

I ran from the room at the first sight of him. The face and the body were grotesque in their disfigurement. Monsters were real. Joseph Merrick was a monster. And to know that he was real. A real-life monster. (I would not come to understand the value of his life until I was an adult.) I ran to the bed my mother and I shared and hid beneath the covers. I had nightmares of him that night. Monsters were real. Thing is, I didn't know that monsters could look like a little black girl like me.

Their name was Warwick. The day they moved into the house two houses down from ours, the neighborhood was abuzz with excitement. Who was this new family that had just moved onto Dunedin? The family was a large one. As soon as you thought you'd seen them all, even more kids would come spilling out from the two-story corner house. There were five kids in the house, three girls and two older boys. Two other older girls had already moved out. What remained were kids that ranged from my age to both of my sisters. It was as if Mrs. Warwick and her husband were having babies every year.

"Lord have mercy!" Ma said, coming inside the apartment, her arms full of groceries, her body drenched with rain. "It's coming down in sheets out there, and those fools are out there watering the grass!"

"Sho nuff?" said Grandma, barely taking her eyes off her cross-stitch pattern.

"I don't want none of you girls messing with that family." Ma had a way of talking to us sternly, as if we were already guilty of a crime. She made her way down the narrow hall toward the kitchen. "You know they got to be high as the goddamned moon, out there watering the grass when it's raining."

I'd never seen anyone high as the moon before. I wanted to go out on our balcony to see what that must look like.

"That's what drugs'll do to you. Make you do dumb stuff like that. Next thing you know they'll be out there trying to plant flowers during a snowstorm."

Ma's lessons were often kamikaze-style like this. There was no sitting down at the dinner table to teach us about life. Instead, her style was to go into impromptu speeches about drugs, sex, alcohol. Ma didn't have any girlfriends so her parental speeches often veered off course into her personal preferences in regards to subjects that were completely inappropriate for young ears.

I have no recollection of my mother having a girlfriend over to chat about her life or men or parenting, or even just plain gossip. Her daughters were her girlfriends. So oftentimes, our life lessons would be tainted by her personal opinions. As the youngest child who worked so hard to emulate my mother, it would be years into adulthood before I could dislodge Ma's personal choices from my own. Her lessons crossed lines of appropriateness, bordered on vulgarity, and should have been labeled with movie ratings: G for General Audience to include Rhonda Ron, as Ma liked to call me; PG for Parental Guidance for Nina and Toya only; or R for restricted to the girlfriends that had yet to cozy up to her hard edges. Ma's sage advice came in the form of little sound bites that she repeated with impunity:

I never let a man give me a drink in a club. Never trust a drink that you didn't see come straight from the bartender, or you'll wake up the next morning feeling like a wet, used washcloth.

I ain't never take no drugs in my life, not even marijuana. You don't know what's in that stuff. Too easy for someone to slip in some PCP. Y'all can mess with them drugs if you want to. You'll be seeing spiders crawling on walls for the rest of your life.

I didn't raise y'all to go to jail. But if you do, I sure hope you make it worth your time. Please don't get caught stealing toothpaste from Woolsworth's. If you're gonna commit a crime, at least make it worthwhile—have a good story to tell while you're in prison. Say you were stealing a diamond from Tiffany's. Least you can do is not embarrass me in front of your cellmates.

If you do end up going to jail you can say good-bye to your mama, 'cuz I ain't coming to visit. I ain't got no business in nobody's jail.

Y'all always dieting. You can go ahead and make yourself an anorexic if you want to. But I'll kill you if you end up dying 'cuz you don't want to eat.

I ain't putting my mouth on no man's penis. Y'all know that's where they urinate from, right?

Y'all might hear that I'm seeing the married man around the corner. I want you to hear it from me instead of out on the streets. And remember this: do as I say, not as I do. I got my reasons.

Our lesson for today was clear: we were not to do drugs. And we were not to associate with the Warwicks. I'd break lesson number two. And in doing so, I'd start our very own Hatfields and McCoys.

10

Be peaceful, be courteous, obey the law, respect everyone;
but if someone puts his hand on you, send him to the
cemetery.

Malcolm X

The Battle with the Warwicks

Stacy and I walked home from school, carefully dodging
puddles of rainwater from the recent showers. It was a cool
fall day, and I was bundled up in my coat. It was a rare
moment when I felt like causing trouble, testing my own
limits, and yet, that's what I felt in the moment. Like a
brazen daredevil, tired of feeling faceless and voiceless.

Maybe my future was to be a badass. There was only one way to find out if I'd be good at it.

"There's the new girl in school," Stacy said, nodding her head to the girl across the street who was headed in the same direction as we were. She was part of the Warwick family. Dee Warwick, the youngest of the clan.

My moment had arrived.

"So what?" I yelled so I could be heard from across the street. I caught the girl's attention. Dee Warwick was my size. What I didn't know at the time was that even though she was about my size, she was about three years older than me—a lifetime considering how young we were. "I don't care about her," I yelled. "She ain't nothing to me."

There was no rhyme or reason for my newly developed bravado. No rhyme in that I had never even remotely attempted to be a bully before that moment. No reason because I had no idea if I could back up my tough talk.

And still, I met the girl's eyes. If I expected to find fear in them I was mistaken. What I saw sent a chill down my back. Dee was amused. And she was game. Dee Warwick was definitely game. And I was a rabbit who'd hopped up nose-to-nose to a sleeping, coiled snake.

"Man, Dre, you better tell that little girl to go on somewhere," Dee said to her older brother. Where'd he come from?

I swallowed hard.

"Why'd you say that?" Stacy whispered to me.

I couldn't come up with a good answer.

"Hey, little girl," Dee said, crossing the street over to my side. "Why you talking to me?"

"Cause I can," I said with decidedly less chutzpah than before.

Dee was in front of me now. A crowd formed around us. Had I thought she was my size? Now that she was close up I could see she was ever-so-slightly taller than me.

"So what you gonna do?" she asked. She smiled as if I were pure amusement to her.

"You'd better get out of my way," I said, trying to imitate my mother's stern voice. Ma could scare me with the ferocity of her voice. Maybe my tone could be equally as ferocious.

"Or what? What you gonna do little girl?"

"Man, Dee," her brother said. "Just knock her out and let's go home."

The next thing I knew we were fighting. I was tough but not nearly as tough as Dee Warwick. She was pure sinewy

70

muscle, a wall I could not get purchase on. The next thing I knew she had me in a headlock, then, as the crowd cheered her on, she flipped me onto the ground, my face in a circle of mud, while she sat on my back.

"Eat it, eat it, eat it," she said.

I could not move. I could barely breathe. I was not only defeated, I was humiliated.

When she tired of torturing me, Dee got up, looked at me and laughed as she and her brother headed home. And I went home too, crying all the way.

"Oh, my God! What happened to you?"

Nina found me sitting on the steps inside our apartment building crying. I was a sad sight. Mud and tears and snot covered my entire face and the front of my coat. I was distraught. I could barely speak. Is this how boxers felt when they got knocked out?

"Rhonda, calm down and tell me what happened."

"She came across the street and beat me up." It wasn't a lie. I'd just started the story in the middle.

"Who?"

"That girl, down the street," I sobbed. "Dee Warwick."

"Oh my God," she said again, very unhelpfully. "Come on, let's get you upstairs and get you cleaned up. We gotta call Ma and tell her what happened."

71

The better answer would have been that she and Toya needed to go out there and defend my honor by kicking some butt. But that wasn't quite the kind of sisters that I had.

"No! No! Don't tell Ma!" I pleaded.

"Calm down. We gotta tell Ma. Wait 'til Grandma sees you. Oh my God, what did she do, lay you in the mud?"

Close, Sherlock, I'd wanted to say. She laid me in the mud, sat on my back and told me to eat it. Which I probably would have done if my face hadn't been smooshed into the ground.

Later, when my mother got home and I'd been cleaned up and appeared my normal, dignified self, the beatdown felt less urgent.

"That doesn't make sense," Ma said as she got undressed. "She came across the street for no reason whatsoever and beat you up?"

She had asked me the question before. What more did she want from me?

"Rhonda?" she pressed. "It doesn't make sense. Now don't let me go down there to that house and make a fool of myself. You'd better tell me the truth and tell it quick."

I told her the facts. All of the facts.

"Oh, so you thought you were gonna be big and bad and pick on someone, and you ended up getting the worst end of it, huh? Well," she said dismissively, "lesson learned."

My family may have been willing to move on, but the Warwicks had other things in mind. Each day on my way home from school, I found a different route to take, for fear of running into Dee. She had seen me in school one day and promised to finish what she'd started. She wasn't done with me? What the hell? Whenever she happened to see me in school, she smacked a fist into her palm, the universal sign for *I am going to kick your ass*. There was no way I was going to suffer the pain and indignity of getting beat up again. My stomach clenched at the sight of her. My knees weakened. It might have been true that I deserved the instant justice for my attempt at bullying. But I didn't deserve the daily mental harassment that followed it. And my fear was real and justified. I'd linger after school, leave out of different entrances, hide in the bathroom, and take onerous routes home—hiding around cars, ducking behind trees, running all the way—in hopes of not getting caught by Dee. This girl was my elephant man come to life. What had started as a childish encounter soon escalated to something far worse.

Fall turned into winter and winter into spring. The Warwicks had made a name for themselves in the neighborhood. Their parents were hard-drinking drug users; the kids were tough-talking fighters who enjoyed the mayhem they caused in the neighborhood. My actions had precipitated a war that was inevitable. They were not in the neighborhood to make friends. They were there to raise hell.

Toya began to be bullied at school by Prissy, Dee's older sister. She, too, was ducking and dodging in an attempt to pass from one class to another. Ma made several visits to both of our schools, explaining to the administrators that we were being harassed by this family.

"Ms. Eason," the principal told my mother, "there's really nothing we can do. Nothing has happened to Toya on school property. If there's an issue between the girls that can't be resolved, you can always move her to a different school."

"Why in hell should I have to move my girls to a different school because these heathens are running around trying to pick a fight with my kids? Toya is a straight-A student in this school."

"And we'd hate to see her leave. But my hands are tied."

"Fine, I'm taking her out of this school and putting her into Northwestern."

The administrator laughed in a way that educated men do when talking to a high-school drop out with little formal education.

"They won't let her in that school. It's not in your district."

"If you and the City of Detroit Board of Education decide to keep my child here and refuse to let her go to a different school of her choice, I'm going to sue the shit out of all you and walk away with your paycheck and theirs! Now watch me!"

When the weather turned cold, there was a rest in the war with the Warwicks. As the snow melted, tempers began to rise again. One day, Prissy picked a fight with Toya while the two were in the girls' bathroom.

"Grandma! What am I supposed to do?" Toya cried into the telephone from the school's administrative office. Ma was at work, and we followed a strict order never to call her there unless the house was on fire. This probably would've qualified as an emergency, but old habits die hard. "Prissy and her girls just jumped me in the bathroom!"

"Sho nuff! What they gonna do about it?"

"I don't know, but I need to come home, Grandma. These girls are denying they did anything to me. I gotta come home. If they catch me after school...."

"Calm down, chil'. Call a taxi. I'll be here waitin' when you get home. I'll pay for the cab, okay? We'll talk to your mommy about it when she gets in from work."

Toya did as Grandma instructed. She got into a taxi bound for home. What she didn't know was that Prissy and her crew had left the school early. They were in front of our house, waiting for Toya, when the taxi pulled up. And they were thirsty for blood.

I sat on the balcony of our apartment, looking at the taxi when it pulled up. Fear had been a constant state of being for me that school semester. I was afraid on my way to school. Afraid when I walked the halls. Afraid when I was on the way home from school. The only place I could relinquish my fear was in our apartment. But the feeling burned inside my gut once again when I saw that taxi pull up. It's one thing to feel helpless for yourself. To see a loved one feel fear and to be powerless to do anything about it reinforced my utter uselessness. And this was all my fault.

The girls pounced on Toya as soon she got out of the cab. I screamed at them from the safety of my balcony as the four girls punched my sister, slapped her around in the middle of the street. They ripped off her blouse, leaving her to fight in just her bra while the neighbors came outside to watch. Toya fought back wildly as they pulled her beautiful long hair to gain a stronghold on her. Finally, she broke free, ran upstairs to the apartment and got a gun I didn't even know we had.

The girls stood outside congratulating themselves for their epic barbarianism. It gave Toya enough time to pull the safety, aim and fire.

Pow!

Pow!

Pow!

My sister stood on the balcony in a bra and jeans, with wild hair and a bruised, tear-streaked face. She shot at the girls as if they were deer and she a famished hunter. The cab driver didn't bother to wait for his fare. He burned rubber and got the hell off of Dunedin as fast as his clunker of a taxi let him, while the girls scattered and ran for their lives.

11

I find it's usually the bullies who are the most insecure.

Tom Felton

Because We Were Pretty

Ma had a decision to make. Her kids' lives were in jeopardy. Hell, the Warwicks' lives were in jeopardy now that Ma discovered she was living with Annie Oakley. Everyone in the house knew about the gun except me. Naturally. But what no one except Ma knew was that it was filled with blanks. Up close they could've done some damage, but at that distance they were pretty harmless. The Warwicks didn't know that. And they probably wouldn't send Ma any thank-you notes if they knew.

To my delight, Uncle had just arrived from Georgia to visit us. Maybe he was hiding from the law again, or maybe he was being a goodwill ambassador. One never knew with him.

"Y'all call the cops?" Uncle asked. I loved being around Uncle. He was very different from Ma. I could hardly believe they had the same parents. Below his thick mustache was a permanent smile that showcased his gapped teeth. He had an easy personality that made you want to hang around him so he could tell you one of his wild tales, like the one of him narrowly escaping the cops while hot wiring a car when he was fifteen. And again when he was thirty. And again when he was—

"No, we didn't call the cops and neither did they. I don't know what to do, Luke. I ain't got the money for a move. If I stay, they gonna kill my kids."

"Not while you got this one around. Girl, where you learn to shoot?" Uncle asked Toya. She sat in stunned silence on the sofa, her hair pulled back in a neat ponytail. Except for a busted lip, there was little evidence as to what had happened to her. But for a person so wrapped up in her looks, that swollen lip may as well have been a tumor. "You ain't hit a damn thing but the concrete. You musta got that shootin' from ya Mama."

Toya half-grinned. She wasn't amused. She had to go to school with Prissy and her crew. This wasn't the end of it.

"They been terrorizing us for months. My girls can't go to the store without having to run from those girls. Or the boys. You'd think boys would be nice to them, but no, they just as mean." Ma pressed her lips together with her fingers. She used to be a smoker. I bet she wanted a smoke right about now. Uncle sure looked like he was enjoying his cigarette, taking long pulls on it and letting the smoke swirl out of his nose. "I'm taking her out of the school. All of 'em. I'm looking for a new, cheap place to stay. I ain't got the time for this."

The dam broke. Every so often, Ma let us see that she really did have tears inside.

"Stop you crying, girl. I got some money that'll help you along."

"No," Ma said, wiping tears from her eyes. "I don't want no money you done stole from somebody, Luke."

"Money is money," he argued. "I ain't never took nothing from nobody that didn't deserve to have it took. What the hell do you care about where it came from? Besides," he said and reached into his pocket. "I ain't steal no money. I been gettin' real hot with the numbers."

Uncle reached into a pocket and pulled out a lottery ticket. He leaned over and handed it to me.

"Here, little girl," he said to me. I'm not sure Uncle ever knew my name. "I bought this while I've been in town. This is for you."

"Is it a winner?" I asked.

"You goddamned right it's a winner. It got about fifty dollars on there."

"For real?"

"For real," Uncle said and took a sip from his can of beer.

Ma said, "I talked to Rhonda's father. He said I need to get a restraining order against that family. I gotta take off work tomorrow and go see about keeping those people away from us."

"Yeah…" Uncle said and nodded. "That's one way to go about it."

"What else am I gonna do? Get out there and start a shoot-out? Ain't it bad enough that we black and poor? Those fools want to go starting a war for no reason as if we ain't bad off enough as is? It don't make no sense to me."

"You want me to talk to them?"

"No. Please. No."

81

"They don't even need to know who I am. This is a four-family building. They don't know who I'm visiting. I'll go have a drink with them over the weekend and let you know what's what."

"Do what you want," Ma said. "In the meantime, my girls ain't going back to school until I get a restraining order against those fools."

Uncle was one of the most charismatic people I'd ever known. He could walk up to strangers and smile and make a new friend without so much as opening his mouth. Apparently, that's what he did with the Warwicks. He sat on their porch on a mild Saturday evening, drank beer and (based on the smell of Uncle's clothes) smoked with Mr. and Mrs. Warwick until the wee hours of the morning. The next morning, Ma roused him off the sofa.

"What'd they say?"

"You gotta wake me so early in the morning, woman?"

"Luke, what'd they say?"

"They don't like y'all. I don't know why. They didn't say. Trust me when I say they weren't full of compliments." Uncle wiped his face with his hand and leaned up on the sofa. "You sure you don't need me to stick around longer? I don't have to get back today."

"No, you can get on back home," Ma said and started for the kitchen. "I'll pray on it."

"Annie," he said, calling her by her childhood nickname. "I think you need something a little more tangible than a prayer. And I think you gonna need something a little stronger than a piece of paper to deal with those people."

Ma turned to face him.

"I got something stronger than a piece of paper, Luke, and I thank you for bringing it with you."

"You know how to use it?"

"Nigga, I'm from the same Georgia backwoods as you."

"Well if your daughter's shooting is any indication—"

"It ain't."

A short time later I sat inside an empty courtroom, talking to a man in a suit about my experience with the Warwicks. We were sitting on the benches, and the man in front of me was turned around, his arm draped casually over the bench while he asked me questions about my experience with them. Was I scared? You bet your business suit I was scared. Did I feel threatened? Um, yeah. The pounding of Dee's fists into her palm while we passed in the hallways

could've been described more as a promise than a threat …
but yes, Mr. Judge, I think it's fair to say I felt threatened.

In the meantime, Ma found a house. She'd come home
saying she'd put rent money down on a two-story house
(two stories!!!! Like a mansion!) on Linwood. Soon
enough, we'd be on our way off Dunedin Street.

A knock on our door. Ma went to the peephole.

"It's their Mama," Ma said.

"Sho 'nuff?" Grandma said. "Lord, what she doing
coming over here?"

"Girls, I need y'all to go to your room."

Ma disappeared into her bedroom and came back with a
long black case. Another knock on the door.

"Just a minute," Ma sang out like she was June Cleaver.

Ma unzipped the case and revealed a shotgun. She
pulled a couple of bullets out of the same magical air she
got the gun, loaded it, and set it on the sofa behind her.
Who was this woman? And what did she do with my bible-
reading mama?

"Girls. Go!"

We scurried to the back. Then the three of us snuck back
up front so we could see whatever bloodshed was about to

happen. We had full confidence that our mother was crazier than any other mother on the block.

"Annie, I wanted to come talk to you," Mrs. Warwick began. "Now why'd you get the law on us?"

"My girls can't go to school without your kids beating them up. I'm sick of your girls picking on my children."

"I know that there's a way we could've handled this without getting the law involved. Your girls are just as much at fault as mine."

"Bullshit. I raise my girls, and I discipline them. I don't let them run wild beating up on people. Prissy and her friends jumped Toya in the school bathroom, and again when she got out of the cab."

"You raise your girls to keep their nose in the air and act like they're better than us and everybody else on this block. You ain't shit like the rest of us. If you were you wouldn't need to be living around here."

"Is that all you came over here to say? Because if so, I'm done with this conversation. I have a restraining order against your family which means I can call the cops right now and have your ass locked up."

"You think you're so big and bad, why don't you step outside so I can whoop your ass?"

Ma backed up, opened the door wide enough for Mrs. Warwick to see inside the house. To see what was lying on the couch. To see what was waiting just for her. Ma placed her hand on her hip. Her eyes said, *Test me.*

"Annette," Mrs. Warwick stuttered. She'd seen the gun. She took two steps back. "You wanted me to see that shotgun, Annette. I ain't gonna hurt you."

"I know damned well you're not."

"You'd shoot me?"

"I'd shoot anybody that messed with me or my kids."

Mrs. Warwick stepped back again, stumbled down the steps, and ran out of the building.

We didn't have trouble with the Warwicks after that day. Not long after, we moved to our green mansion on Linwood.

Twenty years later, Toya called me. She still lived in Michigan while I had set up house in Tampa.

"You are not going to believe who I bumped into today," she said.

"Oprah Winfrey?"

"Very funny. I saw Prissy Warwick. Do you remember her?"

It was so odd how Toya could call that name with such neutrality, as though reciting the name of the long-forgotten high school prom king.

"Uh, yeah, I remember her. Where was she?"

"She's a cashier at Walmart. I happened to get in her line, and her eyes met mine at the same time. I didn't want to get out of line because it would've been awkward."

"You just wanted to prove you're still bold enough to put a cap in her ass."

Toya giggled, not at all ashamed of her moment of unleashed vigilantism. "We chatted for a second, and I asked her why her family terrorized us so much."

"Yeah?" It was a question that I'd often asked myself in vain. "What'd she say?"

"You're not going to believe this," Toya said, stalling.

"What'd she say?"

"She said they bullied us because we were pretty."

"What?" I'm not sure what shocked me more: that our looks were the reason for the harassment or that Prissy admitted to it in the first place.

"Um hmm," Toya continued. "They didn't like us because we were three pretty girls. They were jealous. That's exactly what she said. You remember how Prissy used to wear those bottle-thick glasses? She still has them. And pimples and a Jheri Curl. All these years later."

I was shocked that anyone could look at us as a house with three pretty girls. Toya was the certifiable pretty one. Nina was as average as I. I'd never considered the idea that someone would want to fight us because of our looks.

"She said that? Who admits to that?"

"That's what she said. And most of her siblings are either dead or in prison. You know," Toya paused for a second. "She seems really nice. You wouldn't believe she's the same person who put us through so much hell."

Long after we'd ended the call, I was still stunned. We had been brutally bullied because we were pretty—because *I* was pretty?

Who would have thunk it?

Not I.

Never I.

12

Hope is the word which God has written on the brow of

every man.

Victor Hugo

Movin' On Up

Cold was as constant a companion in our little mint green mansion on Linwood as hope. In winter, the January chill draped itself onto our home like a wet blanket. The cold seeped through thin windows, below uneven doors, down the aged roof, up the decrepit basement and froze our hands and ears and feet.

"I talked to Mrs. Steele," Ma said, as she came in from the outside. She knocked the snow from her boots. She did not remove her coat. I could see her breath when she spoke.

"What'd she say?" Grandma asked.

"She said she'd have somebody come and take a look."

"Lord, she been saying that the past two winters. She ain't gonna do no such thing," Grandma said, herself wrapped in a couple layers of sweaters.

"I can 'bout tell you what the problem is," Ma said. "The furnace isn't big enough to heat a house this size. She bought that thing 'cause it was the cheapest one she could find. But it only heats up a third of the damn house."

Over the holiday, I'd watched *A Christmas Carol*. People might have thought an old meany like Ebenezer Scrooge was fake, but I knew he was as real as my wrinkled, ice cold fingertips. Mrs. Steele was a scrooge if ever there was one. She was an old lady who lived next door to us. Her husband had died years before we'd moved into the house they owned. Talk about rules! I think that lady liked to make rules up just to see if we were desperate enough to abide by them. We were, and—for the most part—we did.

For one, there was no playing on the grass.

"That woman's gotta be out of her damned mind," Ma ranted one summer day after yet another talk about the rules with the landlady. "She said she doesn't want the girls playing on the grass. Rhonda's a kid! Where the hell is she supposed to play? She's so scared about somebody messing up her pristine patch of grass. I'm so sick of getting up every morning and seeing that woman's ass kissing the goddamn sun tending those silly flowers!"

Mrs. Steele was serious about her garden. There was a chain-link fence that enclosed both of our houses together. Somehow, Ma had managed to come up with a truce: I could play in the backyard only. The front lawn was off limits. I sometimes got the impression Mrs. Steele didn't even like seeing us sitting on the front porch—as if we were beat-up old cars propped up on bricks bringing down the property value.

Rule number two, we couldn't have pets.

One day Ma had a grand idea to bring home a puppy. She'd seen it while shopping in the mall and had to have it. It was a white, curly-haired mutt that we named Bingo. We got about two days worth of fun out of Bingo. Then Mrs. Steele saw him. She came out of the house, broomstick in hand—because that's what witches carry—and yelled,

"What's that thing? Get that thing outta my yard. Y'all can't have no dogs over there!"

I scooped Bingo into my arms and went inside to relay the message to Ma.

"You gotta be kidding me!" Ma said when I told her the news. "Well I'll be damned."

Ma went next door to have a conversation with Mrs. Steele. When she came back, she brought with her another compromise.

"She said we can keep the dog," Ma said.

"Yeah! Bingo!"

"But," Ma continued, "she can't see it. Ever. Or hear it barking."

"What?" Grandma asked. "How the dog gonna live if he can't go outside?"

"I shoulda known better," Ma said. "My kids can't get on the lawn so why would she let the dog? But I thought he could at least play in the backyard with Rhonda."

"You gotta give him back, Shirley," Grandma reasoned.

"No!" I said. "I want to keep him."

My sisters had no real interest in the matter. They had no use for four-legged animals when the two-legged ones were far more entertaining. This preoccupation with the opposite sex was starting to create a real wedge between

Ma's relationship with Nina. Soon, it would all come to a dramatic conclusion.

"We'll keep him," Ma decided. "We'll put him in the little room in the basement. He can sleep down there. And we'll carve out a little place for him to pee and poop. And he can play up here with the rest of us, too."

"Who's gonna clean up after him?" Grandma asked, already suspecting she knew the answer.

"We all will, Momma. The dog is a family dog."

As an adult, I always wondered when Ma made promises did she mean them in the moment? Her life contained a trail of broken promises that disappointed people at best, angered them at worst. There'd come a time when her pronouncements would one day be taken as lightly as one takes a vitamin. There was a twenty to eighty percent chance that anything positive would actually come of empty promises.

Grandma had looked doubtful, for good reason. In the end, she had gotten stuck with the task of cleaning Bingo, taking him to the groomers to get him cleaned and shaved. I had all but forgotten about the dog when school was in session. Bingo stayed in the basement so long that everyone except Grandma remembered we had him. Once, when she took him to the groomers, I stood stunned at how thick and matted his hair had become. It was no way for a dog to live. Grandma eventually gave him to a family more interested in having a pet. It'd been a couple weeks before she bothered to inform us that he was gone. No one had noticed.

Ma took Mrs. Steele's rules as fuel to get her own home. A home of our own would have meant the freedom to play on the grass and have a basic necessity like heat in the winter. As a child, I had big dreams of my own too— mansions and limos and fur coats and adoring fans. Most kids dream of living the good life. But my reality was canned soup for dinner when food was running low, and the third of the month (when my mother got her welfare check) was days away. It was hard to fathom how getting off of Linwood could be possible. And yet, the dream pushed Ma forward.

Nina had dreams of her own. She was obsessed with Tony, her son's father. At eighteen, she spent more time following Tony around the neighborhood, keeping up with his whereabouts, establishing her position in his life to any woman dumb enough to want him, than she spent taking care of her child. Nina wasn't exactly college material even though—at Ma's insistence—she'd sporadically attend classes at the community college. One day, Ma would have no more of it. Perhaps she'd seen one too many bruises on Nina. Perhaps watching her own history repeat itself was too nauseating to bear. Whatever the underlying motivation, Ma gathered all of Nina's clothes into a couple of Hefty bags and politely set them on the porch.

"Why are my clothes outside?" Nina asked when she arrived home, after having spent the entire Saturday with Tony.

"You want to be out in those streets running after that no good man, go right ahead. You're eighteen and no longer welcome in my house."

"Ain't nobody running after Tony. I already got him. I don't need to run."

"Fine, Nina. Get out of my house. Take your child and go have a happy life with Tony. And don't call me when Tony starts whacking on you again. You should be focused on your education and improving yourself. I did not raise you girls to tolerate having a man treat you like that, and you can't seem to get enough of that man. And I can't figure out why because he's ugly as homemade sin."

"You are such an evil bitch!"

Now why did Nina have to go and say that? Ma called herself a Christian but make no mistake, she was not of the Dr. Martin Luther King, Jr. variety. She wasn't about to turn any cheeks when a child she birthed called her out of her name.

Ma's eyes bulged. I'm pretty sure she saw nothing but red as she lunged for Nina. At five-three, Nina had a good four inches on Ma, but that fact was of little consequence when Ma laid hands on her. The two were locked in a straight-up street brawl inside the house. Vases broke, lamps fell, Grandma yelled, Toya gasped, my mouth dropped, and my nephew cried at the sight of his mother being the victim of an attempted murder. Ma came to her senses when Nina's eyes bulged as the air left her body courtesy of the powerful hands wrapped around her throat.

When Nina recovered, she had little to say. She grabbed her child and her Hefty bags and went on to find nirvana somewhere else.

After that, life in our home continued as normal. Ma was still a permanent part-time student while juggling work during the day. Toya attended high school during the day while spending the afternoons working in a law office. My retired grandmother and I continued on with our unnatural fascination with hair.

One day as we ate dinner Ma said, "Lord, I hope I get into that nursing program."

We weren't gathered around the same table like a TV family. Being in the same room was the best we could manage. Our family room was crammed with a sofa and chair and a dining room table. We popped a squat wherever we felt most comfortable. I preferred the floor.

"Aren't you almost done with your accounting degree?" Toya asked from the dining room table. "Why would you drop out of school to go back to school?"

"I've always wanted to be a nurse," Ma said. "I want to take care of people."

Ironic, coming from Ma. She wasn't the kind of person I had in mind when it came to nurses. Ma was a woman of little patience. Her tone could be brusque, her mood a pendulum. Whereas my faraway father was an intellect with a laid-back attitude and easy laugh, Ma could be a stubborn drill sergeant who didn't hesitate to use force to get what she wanted.

Ma dropped out of the community college. She had been only a few credits away from getting a degree in accounting. Graduating would have been a real feat for a high school dropout with three kids.

But why would she abandon her degree when she had been so close? Why not get the degree she'd worked so hard to earn? Why move on to another career? When asked, Ma stuck to her personal truth: that she didn't care about that degree—she wanted to be a nurse. The truth may have been more complicated. I think Ma was intimidated by working in corporate America. Her grammar was not quite the King's English. I, little Miss Know-it-All, had not been helpful by constantly correcting her when she mixed up words. She'd say things like "ideal" instead of "idea" or "prosper" instead of "proper," and I wouldn't miss an opportunity to correct her. I wonder now how I made her feel, in my small way trying to make her more like Mrs. Fletcher and less like herself. Had I been partly responsible for chipping away at her already thin self-esteem, furthering the damage inflicted by the citizens of 1950s Georgia? Did she drop out of college because she was afraid of being successful? Did she drop out because she didn't believe she could hack it? Was she going to drop out of nursing school too? Was school a safe haven for her, an excuse not to have to get a professional job as so many conservatives against welfare would have accused? Whatever the true cause of her decision not to finish her bachelor's degree, Ma's decision was final.

"And besides," Ma continued, "I don't have the clothes to work in an office."

"Annette," Grandma interrupted. "I told you Mrs. Steele offered to lend you money so you could get yourself some suits."

"I ain't borrowing a dime from that woman, Momma, so stop telling me about it," Ma snapped. The roles in our household had slowly shifted. Grandma had retired from being a housekeeper, and Ma became the sole breadwinner. Ma had less deference for Grandma than she had when she was a homeless mother standing on Grandma's doorstep begging for shelter. "The government is offering a program where those of us on welfare can go to school for free if we can keep our grades up, and I've already signed up. It's just a matter of getting in."

Finished with her meal, Grandma sat at the dining room table and oiled her scalp. It was a daily ritual. Grandma was constantly oiling her bald scalp. From my earliest memory of her, Grandma had been bald on top, with a smattering of baby fine hair in the back, a la the television character, George Jefferson. Whenever someone decided to put petroleum-based grease in a plastic jar and, on the front of it add buzzwords like *miracle* or *grow* or *super* (and perhaps an exclamation point for added emphasis), my gray-haired granny was handing over her five bucks from her social security check. Every day she was rubbing, massaging and greasing in hopes of regrowing her half-Cherokee half-black hair.

"She ain't ever going to get her hair back," Ma had said to me once, "any more than you're going to have long hair. Ain't no reason going through life wishing for something that's beyond your control. Seems silly to me."

But buying a house was within Ma's control? Did she even know how insurmountable the odds were for her? Maybe Grandma's hair would come back. I wanted it to come back. I was rooting for a sprig of hair to pop up on her head. I wanted to believe that it was within our power to look, be, and have anything we wanted.

Grandma's hair never came back.

Ma was accepted into the government-funded nursing program. For the next year our lives were a very special kind of hell. We had to walk on tiptoe (literally—not a creak could be made from the floorboards or she'd go ballistic). We spoke in whispers and, whenever possible, existed happily on the outside of the house. Otherwise, she'd come barreling out of the upstairs bedroom like a tsunami, yelling, and whooping ass because she couldn't concentrate on her studies.

It was the most miserable year ever to live with Ma—and that's saying a lot about a woman who had mood swings as regularly as other people laughed. She had become a woman possessed—determined to succeed.

The worst of it came at night. I used to share a queen bed with Ma, but since Nina was gone, I'd been promoted and inherited her bedroom. I lay underneath the blankets wearing a sweatsuit and socks and earmuffs. (I'd eventually stop sleeping in earmuffs after awakening one night, gasping for breath after the plastic headband had nearly strangled me to death.) It would seem that just as I'd begun to enter the deepest part of sleep, that's when Ma would start with the music. Marvin Gaye. Diana Ross. Tina Turner. Whatever moved her. She'd lock herself in her bedroom, and at midnight she'd unwind by cranking her stereo as loud as the equipment would allow. She'd play one song, on repeat, into the wee hours of the morning. Knocking on her bedroom door was useless. She couldn't hear the pounding. The walls shook from the bass of the music. Night after endless night, I awakened to the noise, sobbing in my pillow because I was exhausted and needed sleep. Frustrated because I had a test the next morning that I, too, wanted to ace. Toya, the National Honor Society, straight-A high-school student, was pissed. But what could she do? Ma was less concerned with our sleep or our education than she was with her needs. And when she needed to unwind, to hell with everyone else.

What Ma subjected us to was nothing short of music torture—a very real warfare tactic. Playing loud music to hostages as torture is exactly what she had done to us. It was cruel, and it was constant. Music torture was banned by the United Nations. Ma was not the United Nations. She was unrepentant. Her sole focus was on finishing that wickedly difficult school—a feat mastered by only twenty percent of those accepted into the program. She was determined to get off welfare, get out of Mrs. Steele's house, and make a liar out of all those people who'd cursed her as being nothing more than a burden to society.

If achieving her hopes and dreams meant leaving a few psychological scars on her family in her wake, then so be it.

And one day it was over. My helping her with her flashcard quizzes, our not being about to speak or walk or sleep in the house had ended. She made it. Ma graduated. She became a Licensed Practical Nurse, and yes, she bought a house in the suburbs. She hinted at going back to school to become a Registered Nurse, but it never happened. It seemed that the year of intense study had exhausted her will. She'd met her bar and that was good enough— she wasn't interested in raising it higher or moving the goal post farther. There were too many shifts to work, money to be made, mortgage and car notes to be mailed, things and things and more things to buy.

As the years wore on, Ma paid off the three-bedroom ranch style house and lived in it for more than thirty years. Against all the odds, she'd achieved her version of the American Dream.

One day, as an adult, I sat in her home, surrounded by the books, magazines, CDs, yarn, bric-a-brac, and all the other things that made her slowly-acquired hoarder's lifestyle so narrow and shameful. I thought back to that house on Linwood. That house that —despite the invincible roaches—smelled of Pine-Sol and Pledge and rose-scented carpet cleaner. I realized that Ma had never been a housekeeper. She'd never cared about living in a beautiful home—that was aesthetics. She cared about owning a home—no matter what it looked like. She cared about having the thing that others believed she could never possess; having a place no one could ever kick her out of. Her hope had been to prove society wrong. And she had. The squalor and clutter was an accumulation of purchased items that she'd never dreamed of owning—laptops, computers, electronic games, sewing machines, all manner of things meant to heal the still open-wound of poverty.

And yet, no matter how many things she bought to fill the house that hope and hard worked had purchased, it never seemed to be enough to cure what truly ailed her. My guess would be loneliness. But who really knows what haunts another? Sometimes, we don't even know what haunts us.

I still held out hope for Grandma's little sprig to sprout, and my own Rapunzel dreams.

13

There is nothing noble in being superior to your fellow men. True nobility lies in being superior to your former self.

Ernest Hemingway

A Jheri Curl Saved My Life

1983. Michael Jackson's "Billie Jean" was on constant radio play. Lionel Richie was encouraging us to dance all night long. And a new hair sensation (that both of them shared) was riding high in the black community: the Jheri Curl.

Ma decided that I'd start the eighth grade in my new school on the right foot. With the money she'd set aside, she'd taken me to the salon for the very first time to get my hair professionally styled. That had been incredibly exciting for me. Toya, who by this time had a part-time job in a law office via a high school program, made regular visits to the salon to straighten her baby soft curls and experiment with temporary colors (or rinses) that cast dark blue and burgundy tints in her hair.

And now, there I was feeling all shiny and new. I'd entered McMichael middle school hoping for a new life, free of pumping and bullying. Of course, I was intimidated by the idea of going to school with really big kids, some of whom had already turned thirteen. My jazzy outerwear gave me a sense of confidence. I wore brand new Pretty-Plus sized jeans with pink piping on the back pockets and along the side seams that Ma had ordered from the Sears catalog. My matching plaid shirt with ruffles down the front would find itself in the dirty clothes bin after school, not swinging on my head. Had I really done that? Worn my shirt on my head? Yes. Yes I had. And although that may have seemed worrisome to my family, one thing was becoming crystal clear: black women loved hair. It wasn't just me. I was in very good company.

The tide was finally starting to turn. Before my three years were up at McMichael, television would introduce us to female entertainers who took hair to new heights. My mother always had Diana Ross to admire. The impossibly long and thick wig she wore was proof to some in my community that Diana Ross didn't embrace her blackness. Slowly, the sentiment took on a different tone when a brown-skin, statuesque beauty entered the international limelight.

Whitney Houston was my Glam Goddess. She stepped on the scene with a conservative short, teased wig, but by her third video, she rocked a honey blonde wig with curls that made my heart stop. A blonde wig on a black woman was far beyond my scope of imagination. And not one time, as I watched the video, did I get the sense that she was a black woman hankering to be white.

If Whitney made me open my mind to the possibilities of having fun with wigs, Janet Jackson raised the stakes by forcing us to ask the question: is that her real hair? With Diana and Whitney and Tina Turner we knew they were having fun with wigs. Or what we assumed were wigs—maybe they were weaves. Janet, however, changed up the hair game for me. I remembered Janet from the days of being a child actress playing Penny on *Good Times*. From that show, it was obvious that Janet possessed a covetous grade of hair, much like my sister Toya's. Wet it and it looked like she had a Jheri Curl. A 1980s invention, the Jheri Curl was a chemical process that kinky headed girls and boys like me were paying sixty bucks every couple of months (plus maintenance products) to help us manage our naps. So why would someone like Janet—who had naturally beautiful hair—wear fake hair? And what kind of hair was that anyway? Not only was it super sleek, but sometimes it was pulled back so that we could clearly see her hairline. How'd she do that?

It'd be another decade or so before average black women (and celebs of all ethnicities) were following en masse in Janet's footsteps. But what mattered to me during those years in middle school was that I was, at last, normal. My hair no longer set me apart from others. And I discovered that I wasn't the only person who craved a long, beautiful mane.

The chemical process took about two hours. Chemicals and rollers and heat from the dryer combined to give me loose, flyaway curls. I could run down the street and my hair would bounce with every step. I delighted in whipping my head around so that my hair could swing in time. It took years for my hair to gain length, of course. In the beginning, my hair was short and looked more like a wet 'fro. But there was something in the process of having to keep my hair moisturized that made my hair—and other's—grow like a sun-drenched weed.

No longer did I stick out like a dandelion in a green pasture. No more painful comb- outs by my mother. No more burns from hot pressing combs nicking my ears and neck, cooking my skin and leaving dark brown scabs, only to make my straight hair revert back to kinks after a hot summer's day or the passage of time. No more sitting for five hours to get the gazillion braids that I adored. I could walk in the rain or sweat like a sumo wrestler, and my curls would laugh in the face of its enemy.

The professionally-applied Jheri Curl had been a step in the right direction. Everything that has its pros, however, certainly has its cons. My beloved Jheri came with plenty of cons.

Con number one: my hair was … moist. Not sometimes moist. Not kinda moist. Okay, fine. You wanna go with wet? My hair was wet. Always wet. Part of the Jheri Curl maintenance ritual required moisturization. The key to hair growth was moisturize, moisturize, moisturize. In the morning, I applied my moisturizer and activator to keep dryness (and therefore, breakage) at bay, but all friggin' day: wet hair.

Con number two: I had to sleep with a plastic cap on my head every night. How else do you lock in moisture but to put a plastic cap on your greasy head and hope it doesn't slide off and smother you in your sleep? For manageable hair that bounced when I walk? The risk of suffocation was totally worth it.

Oh, and I had to stay away from open flames seeing as my hair was highly flammable and all.

Cons aside, there was another added benefit to wearing my curl. My hair was no longer able to electrify the boys. And the pumping was a thing of the past. Sure, my middle school years included its occasional unwanted butt squeeze here and there, never mind the fact that I'd started wearing oversized shirts that hid my behind—a habit that would stay with me well into adulthood. Still self-conscious about my looks, I regressed deeper into books and tried to deflect attention, while, oddly enough, making strides to gain more.

"Rhonda," Mrs. Dean caught up to me one day after class. "I wanted to talk to you about the honor roll luncheon coming up in a couple weeks."

"Okay," I said. Surely, she was not about to disinvite me to a luncheon that I'd worked so hard to be able to attend. "What's wrong?"

"Nothing's wrong. Why would you assume something is wrong?" she asked with a patient smile.

I shrugged. Guilt was in my blood. I didn't bothering explaining this to Mrs. Dean.

"Anyway, we're having a guest speaker, and we need someone to make the introduction for him. I've heard good things from your English teacher about how well you read aloud. Do you think you'd be able to get up in front a room full of people and read the introduction of our speaker?"

What? Me, in front of a crowd? Obviously she didn't realize that I grew up thinking that I was Whitney Houston in another life. If Whitney could do it…

"Yeah!" I said. "When can I get the introduction so I can start practicing?"

Mrs. Dean smiled, then took a deep breath. "We were supposed to have it already. It's late. As soon as I get it, I'll pass it on to you. You're sure you're up for it?"

I smiled, not sure at all. I'd never been in front of an audience before, not for lack of trying. In elementary school, all of my classmates were heeding the call to audition for glee club. The inner entertainer in me followed suit. Fifteen of us stood in a row and followed the music teacher's lessons. We sang "Twinkle, Twinkle Little Star" as a group. The music teacher kept giving me surreptitious glances. Cool. I was better than I thought I was. A star is born! Take that Ricky and Greg! Then she had us each perform solo.

"Thank you all so much for coming out. I'd like to see each of you here again for another audition soon. I'll let you know when. Uh, um, Rhonda…"

This was it, I thought. The moment the music teacher would tell me, (me!) that out of a group of hopeful singers she wanted me, me, me! To sing lead! Bwahahahaha!

"I don't think your voice is quite … strong enough at the moment for the glee club. I'd like to invite you back here next year to audition. Okay?"

Say what?

As if walking around in life looking like the inspiration for Alfalfa from T*he Little Rascals* wasn't insult enough.

No matter. *That* was elementary, and this was the big time.

"I'm up for it," I assured Mrs. Dean. This was going to be my time to shine. I could feel it in my bones.

Three days before the awards ceremony I still hadn't received the introduction. I had been anxious to get the guest speaker's biography so I could begin memorizing the words. I wanted to look like a professional speaker when I took to the podium, not like some eleven-year-old novice. I wasn't worried about all those people looking up at me either. I was worried about all those people looking up at me while I had to look down to read the introduction word-for-word. I wanted to look back at the room and look them in the eyes as they were wowed by my talent. At least I hoped I had talent. What did I know about being an orator?

"Rhonda," Mrs. Dean called to me as I was walking in the hallway, on my way to the next class. "I'm so sorry this is late, but he finally got it to us." She held the paper out to me. It was a full page of typewritten text. Single-spaced. Ugh! Still, my heart skipped a beat. "Do you think you can do it?"

I nodded, not sure at all.

"You don't have to memorize the whole thing. No one expects that. If you could start off strong, have the first two lines memorized while looking at the audience, that would be great. You can read the rest."

I smiled, already anxious to get home so I could start memorizing my lines. I only had two evenings to learn the text. I didn't have time to worry about anything else. For the rest of my classes that day, I focused on the biography, committing it to memory. I wanted to be like the best speaker I'd ever seen. Reverend Jessie Jackson.

My mother had taken my best friend, Stacy, and me out of middle school early one day. She'd gotten permission from Stacy's mom to take us to see Reverend Jackson speak at Cobo Hall Arena. Ma wanted us to have a foundation of confidence and understand that just because we started out on the bottom, didn't mean we had to stay there. I sat in the crowd, awed by Reverend Jackson. And the words ... the words flowed from his lips like water from a hydrant on a hot summer day, gushing forth with no sign of slowing. He didn't need a piece of paper. He needed the words that were embedded in his head and his heart. I left the arena as awed by the delivery of the message as I was by the message itself: if my mind can conceive it, and my heart can believe it, I know I can achieve it.

Drat! It was not a good sign. All of the honorees stood in line outside of the hall, holding lit candles in our hands as we prepared to proceed in a single-file line into the hall. We were all dressed in our finery. It had taken my mother and me multiple trips to the store to find the perfect dress for me. We'd settled upon a peach silky dress that had a wonderfully full skirt and made me feel like a princess. Ma had gone all out and bought the dress from a pricey department store. My hair was pinned up in a tight roll in the back and in front my Jheri Curl cascaded down the front of my face in an asymmetrical bang. My oversized fashionable eyeglasses capped off the look. I felt as beautiful as ever. And then I saw her. A girl wearing my exact same dress. How could she? We'd spotted each other at the same time as we were getting in line for the processional. And horror upon horror, she and I would both be sitting on stage right next to each other. I had no choice but to shine now. When I got to the microphone, I'd better leave the audience with something to remember me by.

Laughter rippled through the audience like a wave. Yes. She and I were wearing the exact same dress. Yes. It was so cute. The Master of Ceremonies announced that I would be introducing the guest speaker. It was my turn at the mic. Let me get to it already. My stomach flipped, flopped, danced, and jiggled like gelatin. I hadn't expected such nerves. Nor quite so many people in the audience. All eyes on me. I swallowed hard and began.

I knew the words. I added inflections as best I could to staid material. I forced my eyes to stay on the audience. In my head, I was Reverend Jackson. But I looked like Janet Jackson. I was feeling myself—beyond myself.

Then, I was done. As the guest speaker took to the podium, the audience applauded politely. But was it for me or for him? As I passed the speaker, he reached out his hand to shake my hand.

"You were terrific. Really, really good."

Part of me wanted to reply, "Thanks, bud. What took you so long getting that bio to me? You know how much anxiety you caused me?"

But my momma raised me better than that so I just smiled politely, returned his handshake, and took my seat satisfied with my hard work and performance. I'd learned every word, and I nailed it.

"Ladies and gentlemen," he began. "Thank you so much for your warm welcome. I have to say, I was so impressed with this young lady and the way she read that introduction. I was late getting the school my introduction, and did you see how she pulled that off? Can we please take a moment and give Rhonda another round of applause?"

Oh. My. God.

The applause was all for me. I sat there and wondered if I should stand and bow. Or wave. Or what? Instead, I just smiled and looked for my mother's beaming face in the crowd.

It was a heady moment for me. The applause was addictive. I wanted more of that. I decided then that I wanted to be an actress. After years of being teased by boys and ostracized by girls, I found appreciation and acceptance standing in front of strangers, pretending to be someone I wasn't.

I liked being that other person. I wanted to be her forever.

14

Talent is God-given. Be humble. Fame is man-given. Be grateful. Conceit is self-given. Be careful.

John Wooden

Middle School Ego

Beauty is ephemeral. That euphoric feeling you get when you walk out of a salon looking your best is as fleeting as a butterfly. Oh sure, you might be able to catch it once every blue moon, but eventually it'll die. Beauty, like the butterfly, can't be bottled. It can't be held onto forever. The rules of beauty change. The goal post moves, and you find that what you thought you possessed was akin to watching a pre-game show. It wasn't the main event. And what the main event will bring will be even better than anything before it. But you are perpetually in pre-game mode. It was around this time—in middle school—that I began chasing beauty. Except my mode of choice wasn't through cosmetics. Nor was it through any kind of athleticism. If God wanted me to run he'd have stationed pit bulls at my school's exit doors. My mode of choice for finding beauty was through hair. It was out there and when I found it, I'd finally feel—no— I'd finally *be* myself.

I liked middle-school Rhonda. Middle-school Rhonda was a far better version of me than I'd been in elementary school. I had hair that swung! I had boobies! Small, barely there, but definitely boobies! I was learning to accept myself, find my voice, and dish out a butt-kicking or two if the situation warranted. The situation rarely warranted. My peers and I were too busy figuring our way around our new bodies, new periods, new hormones. We didn't have time for beating each other up. Oddly, during this time of finding myself, I'd picked up a new habit that irritated my teachers. I began to write small. Really small. As if I didn't want my words to be seen. As if I wanted someone to make an effort to read what I had to say.

I was a new me, fully feeling Patti LaBelle's anthem with my own new attitude. The girl who got teased for her kinks was blossoming into a young girl with real potential of being pretty. My Jheri Curl had grown long. No longer a short Afro, my curly bangs touched my chin when stretched to their full length. (Length, by the way, was the Holy Grail in the black community, even more sacred than so-called "good" hair texture. Long hair didn't enhance beauty, it *was* beauty and cutting it was damn near sacrilegious.)

Picture me walking to school wearing a short-sleeve white button down shirt, accented with a hot pink skinny tie. My matching white pants had two hot-pink triangular-shaped cutouts on the front thighs the exact same shade as my cotton tie. My shoes? White, of course. One day, I walked to school with Stacy and—so filled with joie de vivre at the new, totally awesome me—I stopped, opened my arms wide like a diva shushing her band while the audience awaited her next high note with breathless rapture and exclaimed, "Oh, I look good!"

Good for an empowering Broadway musical.

Great for a pop song anthem.

Not so great for a girl only months away from an onslaught of tenacious zits. Stacy rolled her eyes. In high school, she'd prove that personality was a far better attractor of friends than whatever the hell I was going through.

What was I going through?

I suspect I'd discovered my ego. I'd found the solution to my hair. And now that I looked as good as, if not better than, some of my middle school counterparts, I wanted them to know that I knew I was no longer an ugly duckling. I had blossomed.

Beauty, in case you missed my point earlier, is as ephemeral as a butterfly. Did you know a butterfly's lifespan is only about one month? My ego trip was slightly longer than that.

But never you mind. High school was right around the corner. There, I'd get my fair share of that bitter-tasting dish better known as humble pie.

15

Progress is impossible without change, and those who
cannot change their minds cannot change anything.
George Bernard Shaw

A Sign From Above

Detroit had three elite college preparatory schools back
then: Renaissance, Martin Luther King, and Cass
Technical High School. Tell any random person with
knowledge of Detroit that you attended one of these
schools and prepare to get a smile and a head nod, a raised
eyebrow and a look of pure appreciation for this
achievement. Or, as was often the case with me, a look of

genuine befuddlement, much like magicians get when they show that no, in fact, they had not chopped the beautiful woman in two after all.

I was no child wonder. However, I did have a certain intellect that served me well. The day every student in middle school tested for the college preparatory schools, the halls buzzed with excitement. The general pressure of taking standardized tests was absent because everyone knew they were able to be enrolled in their local public high school. The test was simply to determine if you'd be able to apply to one of the college prep schools. The competitive spirit in me hoped I'd get into Cass Tech (most likely I'd chosen that school because I liked their school colors: green and white. Later, I'd choose the Air Force over the other military branches because the baby blue shirt and navy skirt appealed to my sense of fashion. Yes, I've always been a deep, analytical thinker.) I was anxious the day I came home from middle school and saw the letter had arrived. Ma wasn't home yet. Grandma handed me the envelope. She stood nearby as I opened it, most likely ready to provide me scripture on defeat and perseverance. I'd have preferred to open it in private so that I could absorb my failure alone before I admitted it to others.

Dear Rhonda Eason,

We are pleased to inform you…

We are pleased to inform you? We are pleased to inform you? Get out! In the history of mail, there has never been and will never be a better opening line than: we are pleased to inform you. Can we agree?

Cass Technical High School (a public school) was pure culture shock. All students new to high school feel like goldfish flailing on sand. But I'd argue that Cass was different from most regular public high schools. As a freshman, my best friend from middle school, Stacy, and I immediately noticed that our brand new Trapper Keeper notebooks and hot pink book bags were not gonna cut it. And despite our efforts to blend in, we'd made a typical freshman mistake: we wore our new school clothes the first week of school. Nobody *ever* wore their new clothes the first week of school. It showed one's eagerness and naiveté. The older kids were too cool to show off their new duds straight away. We were obviously not the cool kids, although Stacy, a quick study with a likable personality, would quickly become one.

Being a freshman at Cass felt as though I'd gone from the minor to the major leagues overnight. The females wore high-heeled shoes and carried Coach purses (engraved with their initials no less) as they traversed past the crammed elevators and up the eight floors of the school building. These girls didn't know the meaning of a bad hair day. Their professionally-maintained coifs and business attire made me feel as if I'd fallen into *A Different World* and every female was Whitley Gilbert.

The guys were no slouches either. What teenage boy wears dress shoes? Suits even? Cass Tech had an abundance of boys who took the "prep" in college preparatory very seriously with their silk ties and suit jackets or button-down shirts beneath V-neck sweaters. I'd just come from a place where kids were dressed like their fashion icons: Salt-N-Pepa and Public Enemy, complete with neon multi-colored leather jackets, sneakers, caps and oversized T-shirts. The kids at Cass might have been the teen version of *Dynasty*.

And there were white people. And Asian people. And Hispanic people. Our school flourished with diversity before the word was popular.

I hammered through the first year at the highly competitive school as many students did—with my nose constantly stuck between two book covers. The difference between me and my ambition-minded companions was that my books were usually authored by Blume or King or Collins or Sheldon.

It was late August when Ma and I were on the porch, waiting for Grandma to come down so we could spend the day at an outdoor farmer's market and bazaar. Ma passed the time eating an ice cream bar. The inordinately high percentage of beautiful beings in my new high school had made me hyper aware of my appearance. Therefore, Ma indulged in ice cream alone now. Her prime years were behind her, but I was still hoping to get my first boyfriend. It was a futile hope.

The novel resting on my thighs was not adequately distracting me from my surroundings. I could feel her eyes on me. Ma did this sometimes. She locked her eyes on me and evaluated without saying a word. In all fairness, I noticed she did this to strangers too, especially if they had even a hint of a health issue. Something as innocuous as a cough would be met with a cold stare and silent diagnosis. Mono? HIV? The big C? Ma was like a two-month old child and I, the embarrassed mother beside her, powerless to distract her from her curious gaze.

At times I flattered myself by thinking that perhaps she was surprised I'd turned out reasonably attractive. But seeing as I was on prescription medicine for the lovely bouquet of ready-to-explode-at-any-moment pimples the heavens gifted upon me, I knew that couldn't be it. Other times I imagined her debating the pros and cons of poisoning my food. Nina and Toya were long gone out of the house, and Grandma was taking more frequent trips down south. With me out of the way, her taste of freedom could become a full-on buffet.

"I'm getting a little tired of seeing you with that Jheri Curl," she said finally.

Ma didn't know how to finesse words so that they landed with a tap instead of a punch. At least this time she rewarded my visual victimization with the cause of her sudden fixation.

I turned to her. "Why? I like it. My hair's grown a lot."

"Yeah, your hair has grown," she said. "But that look is old. It's tired looking."

This from a woman wearing permanent press polyester pants with an elastic waistband from Sears. The thought of giving up my Jheri Curl had never occurred to me. The idea that the hairstyle that had saved me from years of humiliation was just a fad doomed to drift away in time, like my old bell-bottoms, and my one-piece terry cloth short sets and jellyfish sandals was unthinkable. A fad? My activator and moisturizer and plastic cap could someday be—gulp—extinct? An old relic of times gone by? Did Michael Jackson know about this?

Ma said, "I'm making enough money to keep getting your hair done. It won't be like it was when you were in elementary school." Could she sense my dilemma? "And it'll be cheaper than getting that Jheri Curl done." She spoke as though it was a foregone conclusion.

"There's a process to it," she continued. "You'd have to get treatments on your hair to help you transition from the curl to relaxers without your hair coming out."

She wasn't just talking like it was a foregone conclusion; she was talking like she'd done research! Had she caught a glimpse of me this past summer, and while a bead of activator dripped from a lock of my silky curl, fell to my shoulder, collided with my sweat, and slid down my neck, judged me in pure disgust?

Grandma interrupted the moment she came out of the house, all dressed up for our car ride to the farmer's market. She looked like a character out of central casting for a grandmotherly type. A white fake leather purse dangled from her forearm. Grandma wore clear, round plastic glasses that were two sizes too big for her small, hazelnut-shaped face. Today she wore a newer wig, although it was as depressingly obvious as the last—its bright faux gray and tight synthetic curls dared wind, rain, or tsunami to twist it out of shape. I will never be convinced that the creators of *Mama's Family* didn't see my grandmother on one of her jaunts to Georgia and come up with the idea for Vickie Lawrence's character. (If my grandmother were alive today, her heart would be aflutter with joy if she could see how much synthetic wigs have improved over the years. Subtle gray shades, touchably soft fibers, modern short cuts. My mouth is starting to water just thinking about what lies ahead for me at seventy.)

We hopped in the car, a brand new fire-engine red, two-door Ford Festiva. Ma loved that car. It was the first brand new car she'd ever bought herself. She was a terribly nervous driver. I begged Ma to stop honking the horn at passersby. Having acne was embarrassing enough. Having acne while sitting in a car designed for the height-challenged, whose horn sounded like a chihuahua sneezing was more mortification than I could handle.

At the market, I pretended to be distracted by the homemade pies and tchotchkes. It was a nice enough market, not the kind of thing a teenager would typically enjoy, but I'd resolved that I wasn't typical so I delighted in strolling through the homespun goods. No matter how many scented soaps I smelled or knitted scarves I touched, I couldn't hide the fact that I was bothered by the notion that I would someday have to give up the hairstyle that saved my life. I was in high school! This was not the time for experimentation—my reputation was on the line. Okay, fine. No one knew me; hence, I had no reputation. Still, what few acquaintances I did have, I didn't want to alienate because I'd reverted back to the nappy-headed girl who was teased for looking like Buckwheat. No, I wasn't going to give up my curl. Nothing would make me give it up and I didn't care what Ma thought about it. My decision was final.

Something stank. Something in that market smelled like horse manure. The scent strengthened with each step I took through the outdoor market. The tables of the various vendors were side-by-side beneath a large tent. It was a perfect late summer day for the outing, and Ma and Grandma enjoyed themselves as they lingered over spices and taste-tested jams.

"Do you smell that?" Ma asked.

She and I have a nose that could rival any police K-9.

"Yeah," I said. "It's something in this market. It smells like dog poop."

"I feel like it's following us."

Ma stopped, looked around. Whatever it was, she was going to sniff it out. I looked at the bottom of my shoe. She looked in my direction. I couldn't tell if she was looking at the tent above my head or something else. She's so annoying with that staring crap! I dismissed the scent and turned to continue my stroll. Then, without preamble, she erupted into hysterical laughter. I turned to stare at her. Was it something on my behind? Grandma, always down for a good laugh, looked from Ma to me, clearly confused. Ma's hearty laughter grew into an uncontrollable fit. It was so infectious that Grandma began laughing too, her beady gray eyes lost beneath her fat cheeks, while her row of perfectly white dentures gleamed as bright as her teary eyes. They both placed a hand on their distended bellies that bounced beneath their laughter.

Because I suspected that I was part of the joke—most probably the butt of it—I was immune to the humor.

"What is it?" I asked irritably, still smarting from being on the cusp of a major life decision.

"What is it, Annette?" Grandma managed to ask between her own gasps of breath.

"It's Rhonda," Ma finally said, wiping the stream of tears from her face. She pointed to my head.

I touched the top of my head. I felt nothing but … activator?

Ma laughed louder.

Moisturizer?

Tears rolled down Ma's face.

My head's always in a state of wetness, but this wetness felt different … thicker. I pulled my hand away and saw the white thick goo on my fingertip. I was a perplexed city girl who hadn't a clue.

"What is it?" I asked Ma.

"It's birdshit!" she said in raucous laughter. "Child, you can't tell the difference between your hair and birdshit?"

I was more furious than embarrassed. God had all kinds of ways of sending a sign. Not sure why he had to have a bird crap on my 'do' in order to sway me in a new direction.

Obstinate, I still refused to give up on my curl. I resolved to keep my curl until products were no longer sold in any store in America. The Jheri Curl would have to go completely extinct.

Or, I'd have to be completely, publicly humiliated by it.
Whichever came first.

16

The rate at which a person can mature is directly
proportional to the embarrassment he can tolerate.
Douglas Engelbart

ROTC

I surveyed the classroom of other students and thought,
Well. I guess these are my peeps. We were a mishmash of
dorks and geeks and lone riders in our first ROTC class. I
chose ROTC as an extracurricular activity because my
mother wasn't going to spend a cent on uniforms to allow
me to twirl a baton with the majorettes or shake my groove
thang with the pep rally. Cass, even for a mediocre student

like myself, was a grueling exercise in constant study and isolation. I craved female friendships. My mother—a friendless, cynical woman—didn't make it easy for me.

"The more people you have in your life the more problems you have. The best company you could ever have is with yourself."

That philosophy may have worked fine for a woman who preferred to keep her personal life on the QT, but it didn't work so well for a teenager who was trying to actually get a personal life. So ROTC was my only option to meet, mingle, and take a break from the foreign languages that were precalculus and geometry and chemistry.

Out of nowhere, a man not taller than five feet materialized at the front of the class. His fearsome face was wrinkled and pale, and he wore out-of-style oversized square glasses. His highly-starched Army green uniform was laden with colorful ribbons and medals that made him look as if he were ready to walk into a war room and advise the president instead of walking into a room full of sixteen-year-olds with a desire to play military soldiers.

He yelled something that sounded like muffled garble. I had no idea what he said. But the class suddenly sat up straighter in their chairs. I followed suit.

135

"Welcome to ROTC. My name is Sergeant Mancuso." He began to walk down the aisle. He pointed to the first student and yelled that foreign word again. The student repeated it.

What in God's name is going on?

Sergeant Mancuso walked down the aisle looking for the next student to call on. *Please God, don't let it be me.* Why had I signed up for this? I hate new stuff. I hate being in new environments. The possibility of making a complete ass of myself was too great. I liked the familiar, the comfortable, the known. This was an unknown word. An unknown world. And everyone in this classroom seemed to know what the hell this man was saying except me. This was beginning ROTC for heaven's sake. I didn't come from a military family. I had no idea what the hell was going on.

Please, please God, don't let him call on me.

Sergeant Mancuso pointed a finger at another student. With seriousness beyond her years, she yelled out the word. Words? Yes, it was definitely more than one word. I flipped through the pretty extensive lexicon in my head, but these words didn't sound like anything I'd read in a Dean Koontz book.

Sergeant Mancuso turned down my aisle.

If I kept my eyes on the head in front of me instead of looking at him surely he would keep walking by. Why would he call on me anyway? I don't have the kind of face that would stand out in a crowd. My face was completely unmemorable. Right. Of course. I can relax now.

Wait. What? He'd stopped in front of me. I willed my eyes to move. Sergeant Mancuso stood in front of me, his finger pointed accusingly at me. When I'd taken too long to respond, he jabbed his finger in my direction again to make sure I knew that yes, yes, he was pointing at me.

Here goes nothing.

I yelled with spectacular enunciation that would've made Mrs. Fletcher proud, "A tin hut!"

The classroom erupted in laughter. I got that wrong, didn't I? I got it so wrong I couldn't even use my less-than-stellar auditory skills to correctly mimic what they were saying. And the worst part of it all? I still didn't know what the hell the word or words were that I was supposed to be repeating.

"What's your name?" Sergeant Mancuso asked.

"Rhonda Eason," I murmured and looked up at him with eyes that begged for mercy. Strange, but from this distance, the sergeant didn't look so scary. In fact, he appeared amused by my ignorance and cracked a smile.

But I didn't want his smile. I wanted him to keep walking away, go to the next student. Let me stew in my humiliation alone. Because surely, it couldn't get any worse, right? Wrong.

"Private Eason," Sergeant Mancuso looked down at me. "We're gonna make a soldier out of you yet. You wait and see."

Okay, he's done with me, he's about to move along. Soon, I can disappear behind my comforting cloak of anonymity. But the sergeant didn't keep going. I inspired something in him that apparently no other student did. Unfortunately. I inspired him to do the unthinkable.

"You're going to be a general by the time you get out of this class, Eason." Then he reached up, placed his hand on my head and ruffled my hair.

Sergeant Mancuso ruffled my Jheri Curl as though I were friggin' Goldilocks. Didn't he know that you never—NEVER—touch a black woman's hair? White people knew this, right? This was one of those rules that one didn't have to tell because everyone just knew, right? Like not sitting bare-assed on a public toilet seat. Everyone just knows. This wasn't elementary school anymore when I was supplying fake electrical jolts to my male tormentors. I was a woman now, with secrets as to how I came to look—

138

well—like myself. And those secrets could very well be exposed with one ill-placed hand.

"Oh my God, Eason, what the hell do you have on your head?" Sergeant Mancuso pulled back his now wet hand. The class erupted in laughter once more, though I'd like to believe it was less at me and more at his childlike ignorance.

"Ah," he said in (mock?) disgust, wiped his hands and moved away from me. Overall, Sergeant Mancuso seemed pleased with the new crop of enlistees he'd just gotten.

While the class as a whole got through the rest of the hour learning military jargon beyond *attention*, my mind drifted back to my mother.

If her comments about my hair being outdated had been a murmur, and Sergeant Mancuso's ill-advised hand placement was a whisper, then surely, the shout wasn't far behind.

17

I am invisible, understand, simply because people refuse to
see me.

Ralph Ellison

You Talkin' To Me?

English literature. This class was where I belonged. It was
my comfort zone. As I took a seat toward the back of the
room (because that's where all the cool kids sat and I was
determined to blend in), I felt an ease come over me. I was
ready for whatever reading assignment would be thrown
our way: *The Autobiography of Malcolm X, The Catcher in
the Rye, Lord of the Flies.* I was ready to devour, discuss
and dissect.

The class buzzed with students who hadn't seen each other since the year before. Hugs and laughter and high fives all around. I was swept up in the general goodwill around me and, delusional though I was, I felt as though I was some sort of bon vivant, seeing old dear friends for the first time in an eternity.

How mature the girls looked. Classy in their blazers and pumps. I longed to have half the style and grace as any of them. Selena Stillwell walked into the room with the casual confidence of a girl who knew her place in life — and it wasn't at the bottom. My mouth dropped as I watched her enter and take the seat to my left and two desks up. Selena had done the unthinkable. She had cut her hair. She had worn her hair in a popular mullet style, short in front, long and curled under in back. But Selena had taken the drastic step of cutting off her hair at her nape. Now it was shaved smooth in back, short and curled up front.

She looked amazing.

"Selena!" I called cheerfully. I couldn't wait to congratulate her on the bold move of cutting her hair. "Selena!" I called again, louder this time so I could be heard above the roar of the class chattering away.

Selena half turned, as though using psychic powers to determine to whom the voice belonged without actually having to turn around. When she concluded the voice was mine—a person of inconsequential value—she turned her back fully away from me and struck up a conversation with the girl next to her.

Or maybe not. Maybe I was misreading the situation completely. She probably couldn't even hear me.

The person in front of me glanced in my direction, as did the students behind Selena. Talk about embarrassing. Selena was blissfully, willfully deaf to the sound of my voice.

What to do? I didn't want to make a spectacle of myself, but she couldn't keep ignoring me, right? I mean, I was sitting among the popular girls. That made me one of them in a roundabout sort of way.

"Selena!" I called again with bass in my voice this time.

Selena stopped chatting, huffed as though she were an out-of-breath bank robber surrounded by cops, and turned to me.

I smiled and said, "I like your hair!"

Selena didn't look at me so much as she looked right through me, beyond my flesh and blood and bone, and was thoroughly unimpressed with what she found there.

"Thanks," she sniffed haughtily and continued on with her conversation.

I sat there, stunned by her obvious disdain. What was it about me that had put her off? My choice of clothing? My speech pattern? My dark skin? What?

For some inexplicable reason, I heard the lyrics of a Dolly Parton song play in my head.

Two doors down
They're laughin' and drinkin' and havin' a party
Two doors down
They're not aware that I'm around.

No one seemed to notice me. If anyone saw the slight, they acted indifferent. But I felt it. And the humiliation was far beyond Sergeant Mancuso touching my Jheri Curl.

Two doors down
They're laughin' and drinkin' and havin' a party
Two doors down
They're not aware that I'm around.

The incident with Selena was salt in an unhealed wound. Not long before that day, my speech teacher had encouraged me to compete in a regional speaking contest. I did. However, no one in my family could attend. By then everyone had mouths to feed, money to make. Work could not be missed. The days of my mother escorting Toya to spelling bee competitions were gone. I was on my own. My brother-in-law dropped me off at the strange school with a promise to pick me up after the competition. I sat among competitors in a room full of proud parents and families trying hard not to feel sorry for myself. Instead, I focused on each competitor and felt bolstered by the fact that I believed my talent outweighed theirs. When it was my turn, I trudged up the steps in my pretty dress. I was familiar with the "Footprints in the Sand" poem, and though it might have been true that I was walking under the power of His strength, grace and mercy, when I looked out at the sea of unknown faces I felt alone. None were familiar to me. No one was rooting for me.

I won second place. The trophy was almost as big as I was, and yet, the prize felt bittersweet. I stood outside of the school watching families and students head off to their various modes of transportation. I waited for my brother-in-law to return, and I worked hard not to bring my unconscious thoughts into the foreground. I stuffed them down into a dark, muddy place so I wouldn't have to answer the questions that burned inside me. Why wasn't I worthy enough to warrant a day off work? Or, put more simply, why wasn't I worthy?

Selena's blunt dismissal of me solidified my place in her world. In the span of time it took her to turn her back, she communicated to me what I'd always suspected.

I didn't matter.

I was a nobody.

18

Every new beginning comes from some other beginning's
end.

Seneca

Jheri Curl Gone

"You'll have to get three treatments," the stylist said as she
raked her gloriously sharp nails across my scalp as the
shampoo scented the air with a flowery scent. I was at
Charlene's, a popular beauty salon in downtown Detroit. It
was packed that Saturday afternoon, and I was one of many
black women transforming our natural coils into sleek
tresses to copy styles of our cultural icons like Oprah
Winfrey and Anita Baker. "You've got a lot of length. I

don't know how much you had when you started, but this is a nice length."

I wanted to see it for myself. Touch it for myself. It had been years since I'd seen my hair without curl activator and moisturizers weighing it down. Now I savored the process of reinvention. Reinvention. That's the word so often used to describe Madonna. New hair. New makeup. New clothes. New person. New possibilities. Who wouldn't want to reinvent themselves?

It was my time to become someone new. Rhonda, the girl so easily ignored and who blended into the background, was taking on a new persona. As I sat in the stylist's chair through hours of washing, conditioning, drying, cutting, curling, I imagined who I would be when I walked out of the salon. Even if I wasn't the girl with the cheerleader friends and quarterback boyfriend, I'd look like the girl who could *have* the cheerleader friends and quarterback boyfriend. A stranger would not be able to tell the real me from the imagined me because my beautiful, bouncing hair would make me inseparable from those who had it all. If I could look the part, maybe God would bless me enough to win the part. My new hair wasn't so much reinvention as it was camouflage.

The stylist ran the comb through my hair for the last time. Her expert fingers patted my curls. My hair reminded me of Kate Jackson from Charlie's Angels, except whereas she had a center part, I had a part on the side, flipped over the front and curled in the back. The stylist looked in the mirror and said, "Your hair is beautiful."

It was. For the first time in my life my hair was truly beautiful. My hair exceeded my expectations. I couldn't wait to get out into the world and show them all who I was now. And who was I? I was the girl who fit. I fit. I belonged. My edges were bone straight and laid flat, not a hint of African curl to be seen. I shook my thick, shoulder-length hair. The stylist smiled. Beauty was her business, and who wouldn't love it when they got their business exactly right? Another satisfied customer. I was anxious to pay her and be gone, out into the world where my new life could begin.

The minute I stepped in the house my mother covered her mouth as if a Rolls Royce had just pulled up into our non-existent garage.

"Oh my God! Your hair is beautiful. Oh my God! Turn around and let me look at you?"

I twirled. I was proud, as though I had done something that required years of practice and effort, and now I had, upon my crown, my achievement. And my mother was proud. It was as though I'd brought home an Olympic gold medal after years of tryouts and minor league competitions.

"Girl, I better not ever hear you say you want to cut your hair, you hear me? Your hair is beautiful. Don't let them scissor-happy beauticians start whacking on it."

"I won't," I said, promising to be gentle with my crowning achievement.

"God, I'm so glad you got that Jheri Curl. Talk about money well spent."

Everyone was home. As fingers touched my hair, compliments touched my soul. I was like the rest of the women in my family now with straight, manageable hair and a burgeoning beauty I didn't know I possessed.

Over the next few months, I discovered a newfound love for my hair. And, oh, the hair products. My particular favorite was Bone Strait by TCB. It came in a tan bottle and was true to its word. After washing and conditioning my hair, I could blow dry my hair bone straight and dance around with hair that looked exactly like Jermaine Stewart's, the singer most known for the hit song, "We Don't Have to Take Our Clothes Off." I experienced a feeling of wholeness that I hoped would last for the rest of my life.

19

The fool doth think he is wise, but the wise man knows
himself to be a fool.

Shakespeare, As You Like It, Act V. Sc 1.

All Natural

My grandmother watched me prance around the house every weekend, experimenting with my new, glorious head of hair.

"Keep it up and you're going to end up as bald as a baby's behind," Grandma warned.

"Grandma," I explained calmly. "I'm not going to take out my hair. I heard Oprah say that she washes her hair *every* week, not every other week."

Grandma sat in the plastic-covered chair engrossed in a Search-A-Word puzzle.

"Every week is too often."

"But Oprah does it," I repeated. Didn't she hear me? Maybe Grandma didn't have her hearing aid turned up high enough. "And she doesn't put oil in her hair either. That's how she gets her hair so bouncy."

Grandma looked up at me. "Chil', you ain't using good common sense. You got Negro hair. You don't need to be washing your hair every week, and you got dry hair. Your hair needs oil."

Did Grandma even know who Oprah was? She watched her every afternoon.

"Grandma," I explained with the patience of a priest. "This is what Oprah does."

"Chil', Oprah got a million dollars and a professional who does her hair. You ain't got nobody to do your hair every week. You gonna take your fool hair out of your head."

What could Oprah's stylist, Andre Walker, possibly know about hair that I didn't know? Okay, fine. He knew a

152

lot more. My teenage ego would give him that. But there wasn't a whole lot of science to washing, conditioning, and drying. I ignored Grandma because Oprah was, indeed, a Negro. As was I. If once a week washings and no oil were good enough for her, then dammit, it was good enough for me. Am I right?

I'd gotten some money from somewhere. I have no idea where as I'd never gotten an allowance as a kid. Perhaps it was leftover from a Christmas gift. I ventured to the mall to look at all the stuff I still didn't have enough money to buy.

"Excuse me, Miss. Would you like to try our new hair products?"

I walked over to the woman who was standing behind a long table covered with bottles and jars from a company I'd never heard of.

"What's this?"

"This is a new all-natural hair product line for women of color."

I examined the bottles. To a girl who desired long, beautiful hair above all else, the plastic bottles might as well have been covered in magical fairy dust.

"All-natural?"

"Yes. Perms are so hard on the hair. In time, it'll start to thin your hair. This line of all-natural hair care products was designed especially for women of color." She ran a hand through her luscious, thick mane. "This is the only product I use on my hair. We have an entire line, including relaxers, shampoos, and conditioners."

"Really?" I felt the budding excitement begin to grow inside me at the idea of having hair as straight and voluminous as hers. Mind you, my shoulder-length hair that had been revitalized thanks to the Jheri Curl was beautiful. I knew that. But weren't there degrees of beauty? Wasn't there always a higher level to be achieved? My shoulder-length hair was cool, but having hair down my back would be cooler.

"Will this make my hair grow?" I asked.

"Of course. That's the benefit of all-natural products. It comes from nature and is designed to work in conjunction with your natural Ph balance."

That was all gobbledygook to me. The main point was that it was going to make my hair grow, and I knew this to be true because she had wonderfully long hair and people didn't promote products they didn't actually use. Right?

It was completely unnatural of me to use logic or restraint when it came to my hair. Therefore, it was only the size of my budget that prevented me from buying the relaxer kit. All I could afford was the shampoo and conditioner. Next time, I'd definitely buy the relaxer kit because *that's* where the real magic happened.

I wished the city bus would move faster as I could hardly wait to get back to the house and try out my new shampoo and conditioner. Oprah probably already used this stuff. Rich people always got the good stuff first. Grandma didn't know anything about that kind of thing. She hailed from a tiny little dot on the map called Statesboro, Georgia. This was Detroit, and Oprah lived in Chicago. Big city women had big city ideas, and I was one of them. I couldn't wait to see Grandma's face when my weekly hair washes with my all-natural shampoo made my hair grow down my back. Having the last laugh would be fun, fun, fun!

"Look at what I got," I said to Grandma when I got back to the house.

Grandma, a balding woman obsessed with regrowth, couldn't help but have her interest piqued. She was as obsessed with hair as I was, and she showed more than mild interest in the products.

"It's all natural. And Ph balanced for my body type," I recited as best as I could remember. The details weren't really the point; it was the results that mattered.

"Sho 'nuff?" she said, turning the bottle in her hand with more than a passing curiosity.

"I'm going to wash my hair."

"You just washed your hair yesterday."

"Grandma, there's no such thing as hair being too clean."

I went into the bathroom and lathered up.

Hmm…. This was different.

Not good different.

Bad different.

Very, very bad different.

As soon as the shampoo formed a lather in my hair, I knew there was something wrong. My hair stuck together like I'd put glue in it. What was in this stuff? I washed it out and figured it was part of the process. I would *not* tell Grandma about this little mishap. All I needed was a little conditioner to detangle my hair. Although detangle wasn't quite the correct word here. Un-mat my hair was a better description. I applied the conditioner on my hair liberally.

Oh… my….

"Grandma!" I called. "Grandma!"

I heard her tiny feet scurrying to the back of our ranch house.

"What's the matter with you, chil'?"

"My hair is all stuck together."

"Sho 'nuff?"

Grandma didn't have the most extensive vocabulary. What she did have was a sense of humor and a penchant for laughter. And so she laughed. Like, *a lot. Too much.* How could she be so cruel? Didn't she see the dire straits I was in?

"What am I supposed to do?"

In between hiccups of laughter, she said, "Try washing that mess out with your regular shampoo. Lord, what they put in that bottle?"

"That lady said it was all natural," I said, reaching for the bottle of Suave shampoo.

"Yeah, well, horse manure is all natural too, but I wouldn't put it in my hair."

After that incident, I decided to cool my heels when it came to washing my hair every week—especially with shady products being hawked at now-you-see-it-now-you-don't booths at the mall.

20

Envy blinds men and makes it impossible for them to think
clearly.

Malcolm X

The Bad Cut

I couldn't help but stare at Selena Stillwell during class. I
studied her with the intensity of a student vying for magna
cum laude in stalking. I memorized the cut of her hair,
envied her naturally lithe frame, despised her aloofness,
and marveled at her popularity. She had it all: friends,
beauty, and style beyond any I'd known before. She was
Halle Berry before the world knew Halle Berry, and how
could you not fixate on a person like that? I was fascinated

by Selena's ability to be beautiful and confident with only two inches or less of hair. She clearly didn't believe that hair defined her, and she was right. She was a knockout without it. How could you not want to live in her shoes for a day and feel the envious eyes of admirers around you? And then it hit me. The only thing standing between me and what Selena possessed was a pair of scissors.

The salon, a spacious and glamorous shop, bustled with activity. I and five others sat in the front of the salon with a bird's eye view of the entire place. It was customary to sit for an hour or more in the shop, just waiting to get in a stylist's chair. And I didn't have an appointment either. I was a walk-in willing to take my chances with whomever I happened to get. I was pretty confident God would steer me in the right direction. I'd been without my Jheri Curl for about five months at this point. Now, after a week of contemplation and months of envying Selena, I'd made the huge decision to cut off my hard-won six inches of hair the week before, and was willing to leave the task to anyone with a license. Or without a license. I mean, really. Whoever checks to see if their stylist has a valid license? It's one of those things we blindly trust in, like chefs washing their hands before cooking. Who really knows? I was confident that I'd get the beautician with the magical sheers who'd transform my hair into a sleek, modern cut, thereby making me the edgy "It" girl I believed lived inside me. Ma gave me the money to get my hair done. She had no idea I was going to cut my hair. She was going to be so surprised when she saw the new me. My leg bounced anxiously. I was ready to do this!

"Rhonda?"

"Yes?" I said to the effeminate looking guy standing behind the counter.

"You're with me, honey."

I sat glued to my chair. Is he for real? No, he's not. This guy must be the shampooer. He's not ... he can't be....

He was.

This will be okay, I assured myself as he led me to the washbowl. His washing technique was clumsy. I wiped droplets of splattered shampoo from my face. He's fine. What's a little shampoo? Hey, Oprah has a guy who does her hair. And Oprah was definitely the High Priestess of hair in the black community, what with her layered haircuts that flipped and flopped and flung in every direction. If a guy did that for her, surely this guy could manage a simple haircut.

With a sopping wet and fully conditioned head, I was led back to his chair.

"Okay, honey, how do you want it cut?"

"Short, all around." I said.

"You mean like Jamie Lee Curtis in *Perfect*?"

Hmm ... without a picture it was tricky to get my point across.

"Shorter and pouffier in back," I said. "Like Anita Baker."

"Oh, I love her cut."

He got it. He totally got it. See? No worries. I was going to look fantastic! I settled back into the chair as he proceeded to take out his sheers.

"You're not going to dry my hair first?" I asked.

"I prefer to cut hair wet. Don't worry, sweetie," he said, sensing my trepidation. "Everything's going to be just fine."

I sat with the nylon cape draped around me. Looking at my head, distended above my body, reminded me of a doll I got at Christmas when I was a kid. Ma had finally wised up and realized that I couldn't care less about Barbie and Ken or making up a fictitious life for them to lead. I didn't believe in fairytales. I believed in hair. The year I broke my new Barbie on Christmas Day must have been when Ma realized what I valued above all. The next Christmas she got me a doll's head. It was a dark brown doll's head propped onto a hot pink plastic base. It was the best present ever! Unfortunately, I didn't grow up to be particularly adept at styling hair. But my love for that doll's head and the Cleopatra haircut she came with gave me hours of pleasure.

While I was busy reminiscing about the good ol' days, Mr. Happy Shears was busy whacking off my hair. I had no idea how the process was going. I had, after all, basically asked him to cut me almost bald. And from the looks of things, he was doing exactly that.

After the shears came the clippers, with its ominous buzzing sound. I felt the teeth rake against my bare skin, erasing the hair that remained in the back of my head. My kitchen had been the source of so much pain for me all those years ago. Wasn't I afraid to go through that again, when the hair started to grow back? Wasn't I afraid of having my real kinks show as the hair would start to regrow? No, I wasn't. The confidence in my newfound cooperative grade of hair made me all but forget about the little girl with the electrifying coils.

"How do you want it styled?" he asked.

"Straight down, all around," I said.

Mr. Happy Shears made my hair sopping wet again by applying enough liquid products to fill a dam. Then he started with the blow dryer, which he wielded like it was a hand-held fan giving cooling pleasure to my tender scalp; except it wasn't a hand-held fan giving cooling pleasure to my tender scalp. It was an electric blowtorch blowing a gazillion watts of heat at me and burning the hell out of my scalp.

"Sorry," he said as I jumped when the heat nearly burned the scalp from my head.

Mercifully, my hair was finally dried. And my hair was cut—short. So super short. And, well, did I like it? It wasn't bad. I didn't think. Well, maybe after he finished curling it I'd see it was exactly like Selena's. Or, dare I hope? Even better.

Mr. Happy Shears greased my hair with Blue Magic while the curling tongs heated in the old-fashioned steel stove.

I hated those curling irons. No matter how many times I got my hair pressed as a kid, I could never get past having a thick piece of metal—so hot that smoke streamed from it in big wafts like fog on a misty river—get so close to my skin. It was a weapon far more dangerous than a hot electric iron could ever hope to be. Mr. Happy Shears began curling sections of my hair, getting a little too close for comfort for my liking.

I yelled out an expletive as hot as the iron that skimmed my ear. The entire salon turned to look at me.

The stylist backed away from me, not knowing if I'd cuss him out, storm out of the shop, or apologize profusely and settle back down.

The steam I imagined coming out of my nose was comparable to the steam wafting off his hot iron. I wanted to grab it from him and stick it up his—

"I'm sorry," he said. "It's just a nick. I got a little too close."

That's when it hit me. It wasn't the fact that he was a man that should've distressed me. It was the fact that this tenderfoot was probably two days out of beauty school.

I eased back in the chair—as nice girls do—and held my breath for the rest of our session. I was so angry I couldn't see myself, my hair, or the other patrons. All I could think about was my own rage at being branded like a cow in a professional establishment.

Finally, Mr. Happy Shears used the rake comb to style my hair. I gathered the presence-of-mind to snap back into the moment and look into the mirror.

My mouth dropped.

His brows rose. Mr. Happy Shears patted the back of my head.

"You like it?" he asked, as though not sure he did and was looking for a second opinion.

I was speechless. The other stylists spied on his work through their mirrors. A few bolder beauticians turned around to check out the lopsided steaming heap of curled shit on my head.

"It's fine," I said, because that's what nice people say, but my clipped tone and stony face certainly belied my words. I yanked off the nylon cape and stalked toward the cashier without tipping Mr. Happy Shears.

I walked out of the salon thinking, *Oh, God, what have I done?*

The bus ride home could have been so much longer. I would've appreciated a slow, circuitous route, maybe veering off of Grand River, doubling back over to Telegraph and taking I-96 toward Chicago then hitting the I-90 up toward Wisconsin, then over to Minneapolis where I'd stop in to Paisley Park and cry purple tears on Prince's shoulder.

"All I wanted," I'd sob between sips of grape Kool-Aid, "was a haircut not all that different from yours on the cover of your *Controversy* album. Oh, Prince. How do I go to school with this lopsided, uneven, boxy mess instead?"

"You got the look," he'd reply as he stroked his chest hairs. Prince, in my imagination, liked to lounge shirtless on his purple chaise, with tight purple pants and high-heeled boots.

"Really?" Was it possible that maybe I was in shock at the severity of the new haircut, and it wasn't as bad as I thought it was? "Wait, isn't that a song with you and Sheena Easton? Hey, she sorta has the haircut in that video that I was aiming for. I wish her stylist had cut my hair."

"I could never take the place of your man."

"Anybody could take the place of Mr. Happy Shears. Hold on, does that mean you cut Sheena Easton's hair?" He'd lick his lips and smile suggestively. "You did not! You're so silly."

"Delirious."

"Yeah, that's what my mother's gonna be when she sees I cut it off. I cut it all off. Years of growth. And I have to go to school like this. I wish I could cover it up with something."

"Raspberry beret."

"Thanks, but no."

"I'd better get home and face the music. Ma is gonna—"

"Bat dance."

"Kill me," I'd reply.

"Sign of the times," he replied. "Sign of the times."

But the Grand River bus didn't head out of town. Instead, it dumped me off at 7 Mile Road. I got off and headed home. When I got there, Nina and Toya were over.

"You cut your hair?" Toya exclaimed.

"Yeah," I said.

Nina said, "It looks nice, turn around."

I turned around with a smile pasted on my face, non-verbally communicating to them the direction I wanted this conversation to go.

"It's nice," Toya said. "I can't believe you cut your hair."

Ma walked into the room. "Oh my God!"

Here's the thing about Ma: she doesn't have much skill when it comes to being gentle with other people's emotions. She doesn't know how to handle with care. She says what she thinks, and if you can take it, great, if you can't, well, that's what therapists are for.

"What in God's name did you do to your hair?"

Let me take another second here to explain my mother's facial expression. Imagine you're sitting on the toilet in a gas station bathroom (don't worry—you're using a double-layer of toilet seat covers). Suddenly a man wearing a Jason mask, you know, from those *Friday the 13th* movies kicks in the door. He wields a blood-stained chainsaw above his head. Hey, remember those toilet seat covers I said you were using? Well, you're not. So. Gas station. Your ass. Bare toilet seat. Jason. Bloody chainsaw. Got that facial expression burned into your brain? Yeah, that's a notch below what my mother's face looked like in that moment.

"You don't like it?" Nina asked.

"No," Ma screeched. "No, I don't like it at all. It looks terrible! Turn around."

I turned sans the smile I had the last time.

"Oh my God," she said as though hearing a young neighbor had just died in his sleep. *And he was so young ... such a shame* type of a way. "All that money we put into growing out your hair, and this is what you did to it."

"Ma," Toya said, "it's only hair. It grows back."

"All my money, thrown away. Your hair is your crown. Why would you spend all that time and money growing your hair just to cut it off? I don't understand."

Ma shook her head and left the room.

"Rhonda, ignore Ma," Toya said. "She's old school. Your hair is nice." Then she added, "It'll grow back."

"She's so insensitive," Nina said. "I'm so glad I don't have to live with her anymore."

"Me too," echoed Toya.

My obsession with hair began long before that moment, but something about that time period sparked a desire for change in me. When I had my Jheri Curl I didn't want to give it up for all the gold in the world. And then it was gone, thereby sparking an insatiable need to find the perfect hairstyle that could encapsulate who I was as a person.

Of course, finding a hairstyle that expresses who you are is difficult when you have yet to figure out that part of the equation.

21

The best way to escape from a problem is to solve it.

Anonymous

On My Own

There is no better place to discover what you're made of than in the military. I joined the military not because I wanted to know what I was made of; I was certain my head was filled with nothing but twelve-inches of coconut-scented curls. Neither did I join because of a noble cause to serve my country. (If I ever run for political office, remind me to re-edit this book and delete that sentence.) Instead, it came about from a desire not to commit matricide.

There comes a time in every teenager's life when they feel a deep-to-the-marrow urgency to get the hell out of their parent's house. I felt it many times over. The first time was the summer I was transitioning from middle school to high school. I was excited to start going to Cass Tech and even more so when my admission paperwork arrived at the house.

"I get to choose a major!" I said excitedly, flipping through the small booklet. "I'm going to major in drama, then go to the University of Detroit at Mercy and major in drama there, too."

"No, you ain't." Ma said casually. "You're going to major in business."

I looked back at the form. Sure enough, there was a major for business administration.

"I don't want to go into business, though. I'm an artsy person. I want to be an actress."

"Rhonda, you like eating, don't you? You're not about to go to school and major in acting and then get out into the real world and can't get a job. If you don't have any skills, then what?"

"I'll get a job," I replied, albeit, not wholly convinced myself. "Or I can major in drama and minor in business administration."

"You're going to major in business," she said with finality, her fingers never missing a loop on her crocheting.

"I'm the one who has to do the work," I reasoned, "I should be able to pick what I spend my time studying."

"I'm not arguing with you, Rhonda. You're going to do as I say or get out of my house."

There was always that lingering threat that my living in her home was a gratuity she provided me instead of a lawful requirement. I resented the threat of homelessness. To me, it was tantamount to holding someone as your emotional hostage—telling them, "Do what I say and I'll love you. Don't, and I won't."

Ma continued her reasoning, "As long as you know how to type you'll always have a job. No matter how much technology comes about, businessmen will always need a secretary."

That was my mother's highest ambition for me. To be a secretary. The desire to leave her house hit me with startling force. There was a time I wanted nothing more than to fly beneath her wing, to echo her voice, to enforce her rules. But now I was coming into my own and seeing my mother as less of a mentor and more as an excuse to pop Excedrin by the bottle. Comments like the one she'd made about me always being able to have a job as long as I could type made me adore my long-distance father even more than I already did.

My father (and that's what I always called him—even in his presence—never Dad, never James, just *my father* or nothing at all) had lived in New Jersey—where he'd been in the military and met my civilian-worker mother. My father had tried living with Ma, playing dad to me, and stepdad to my sisters. But he was from Mars and Ma was from Venus, and they couldn't seem to find common ground on Earth. He'd left my mother before I could make it out of diapers. The advent of their relationship always befuddled me. She was attracted to his handsomeness and his intellect. He was attracted to her determined spirit and … well, I'm not sure what else. My mother, as I've said before, has a lot of sharp edges. My father was the exact opposite. If Ma was cocaine, my father was weed. If Ma was a shot of whiskey, my father was a wine cooler. Same category, different effects.

With a deep desire to succeed, my father returned to his childhood home of Pittsburgh to begin his career as a newspaper journalist. Oh, how my mother mocked him to me for being a *grown ass man* still living at home with Mommy. All the condescension couldn't dull the brightness of his star in my eyes. Each summer he'd send me a ticket so I could hop a plane to visit with him. It was the highlight of my youth. With each passing year, as my mother worked hard to lift herself out of the welfare system and into a nursing career of her own, my father was working hard, too, beginning a long career in print journalism. His struggle ended quicker than hers, as is often the case with men. My mother became bitterer when she discovered he was marrying a college-educated woman with an MBA ... in mathematics. And together, they were moving on up into a sprawling five-bedroom abode in a ritzy New Jersey neighborhood with a new little girl in their future.

It was my father's fault that I dared to dream of being a professional actress, that I was ready to risk my life on the hunch that I could stand on the Academy's stage with an Oscar in my hand. He taught me to dream bigger dreams. As with every kid, I changed my future profession as often as I changed my socks. My father challenged not some of my choices but all of them. When I'd say I wanted to be a flight attendant, he'd ask, why not a pilot? When I told him I wanted to be a lawyer, he'd ask, why not a judge? When I told him I wanted to be a journalist, he didn't take it as a compliment that I wanted to walk in his shoes. Instead, he said, "Instead of being the person who has to run out and

174

beg someone for an interview, why not be the person that reporters are vying to interview. Why not strive to be a person of noted accomplishment?" (Katie Couric might take exception to this way of thinking, but I got it.) And my father wasn't joking either. He wanted to know why I wasn't aiming for the moon, and at worst, if I failed, I'd land among the stars. If that sounds familiar, it's because it's derived from a quote he'd jacked from Norman Vincent Peale and wrote in a card for me. My father and I were like-minded people. And, unlike Ma, he could see the value of throwing caution and reason to the wind and living out your heart's desire.

But my father wasn't here. And my mother didn't give a flying fig about my heart's desire. She wanted to make sure when I was out of her house—I'd be out of her house forever, and she made no bones about saying so.

Although my father was only a phone call away, I couldn't call him. I had an unconscious stubbornness when it came to reaching out to him for what I perceived as a favor. Despite my reverence of him, there was an emotional duality in my feelings. In my head there was an 'us' against 'them' mentality. 'Us' being my mother and sisters, and 'them' being my father, his new wife, and daughter. It wasn't until I was an adult and away from my mother that I realized this mentality was not something I'd imagined but an idea covertly implanted in my head through my mother's machinations. Ma needed people on her team. She said as much years later when she got into an argument with her sister, and her kids sided with her sister—our aunt. My mother was furious at us for our treasonous behavior.

"I need people on my team! My side! You're my daughters; you're supposed to be with me! With me!"

I'd always been on my mother's side as a child. I was happy to burrow myself into her lap, align myself with whatever position she took. She was my mother, my caretaker, my nurse, my cook, my landlord, and as such, she was always right.

Except when she wasn't. And as a teenager I began to see Ma as an antihero. A pure, pulsating pain. The kind of pain that a pill couldn't alleviate. The kind of pain that a doctor can't see on an X-Ray machine. The kind of pain that could only be alleviated through separation.

When I enrolled in Cass, I majored in business, because I still needed my landlord. Four years later, in the spring of 1991, I was preparing to graduate. I'd done respectably on my ACTs, but I'd totally bombed my SATs. Harvard was out of the question. Even though I wasn't Ivy League material, college was still a must.

Once again, in March, dangerously close to graduation day, I sat on the sofa and told Ma my plans.

"I want to stay home for the next four years and go to U of D." I hadn't applied. It was probably too late. Part of me probably knew this was out of the question.

"Rhonda. I've spent my whole life raising kids. I'm ready to have all y'all out of the house now."

"But I don't have anywhere to go. I need to go to college."

"You'll need to figure that out. Ask your father to help you."

I can't, I wanted to say. You've established an Us-vs-Them mentality in my head. You've instilled the whole black-women-have-pride thing in my head. If I go to my dad—rational though that might be—it would be like asking the enemy for a loan.

"Ma," I said, incredulous that my mother was basically giving me an eviction notice at seventeen years of age. "I need to go to college."

"I'm not saying that you can't. I'm saying I'm not paying for it. I'm not co-signing a loan and you need to be out of here after you graduate."

In that moment, I truly hated her. Not just disagreed with her. I hated her. What kind of mother wouldn't let their child—their obedient, friendless, socially-deprived child—stay home so they could go to college?

"Fine," I said. I was my mother's kid: strong, resilient, independent. If she wasn't going to help me, I'd help myself.

In less than four months, I packed up my hot curlers and grease and got on a plane bound for San Antonio, Texas. I arrived in The Lone Star State in August where the unseasonably cool weather dipped below sixty degrees. I stood at attention, my petite body shivering in shorts and a tank top while the woman in front of me yelled in no uncertain terms that she was my momma now.

22

You're imperfect, and you're wired for struggle, but you are
worthy of love and belonging.

Brené Brown

The Military Years

Basic training was stressful enough without me having to
worry about my hair. So I didn't. My awful short cut had
grown out long enough over the previous year-and-a-half
for me to be able to slick my relaxed hair back into a
ponytail. Turns out that a slicked back ponytail was a good
look on me. During the summer of 1991, I'd dieted my

five-foot-two chubby frame down to one hundred and eleven pounds by eating a diet that consisted of one piece of unbuttered toast and a grapefruit for breakfast; a diet Pepsi and salad for lunch, and whatever Grandma cooked for dinner. In preparation for my August enlistment, I power walked for an hour every day while listening to Janet Jackson's *Rhythm Nation* on my CD player. I didn't want to have to worry about keeping up with the workouts any more than I wanted to stress about how to maintain a haircut.

My training instructor (or T.I.) was a rail thin white woman with an outdated curly perm and a pinched, humorless face. I remember the day she walked past each of us scared airmen—still dressed as civilians—standing at attention at the foot of our assigned beds as she went over the rules that we'd abide by for the next six weeks of our miserable lives.

"You will get up the second Reveille plays over that loud speaker. You divas will not linger in bed as if this is a goddamned Texan spa. This ain't no spa, and you don't have no snooze buttons. You got that, airmen?"

"Ma'am, yes ma'am!"

Tech Sgt. McClendon walked down the bay, looking at us in disgust, as if she were offended that this was the best bunch of women the Air Force could deliver. Her battle dress uniform was heavily starched and pressed so that the sharp creases down her arms and legs looked like deadly weapons. Tech Sgt. McClendon's boots were so shiny they might as well have been coated with liquid glass. Beneath her skinny arms was a wide-brimmed hat that, on her head, called to mind Gunnery Sergeant Hartman from *Full Metal Jacket*.

"You will get in the shower every day. You will not skip a shower so that you can get more sleep. Do you understand me?"

"Ma'am, yes ma'am!"

Every word from Tech Sgt. McClendon was yelled and echoed through the hollow bay. "You will spend no more than five minutes in the shower, and there will be a monitor at the door, with a timer to call five of you in the shower at a time and will make sure your lazy asses don't linger in the shower for more than five minutes. Am I making myself clear?"

"Ma'am, yes ma'am!"

"White girls." She was identifying pretty much everyone in the room except me and a friend of mine who, as it happens, also came from Cass and travelled on the same plane and bus as me to Lackland. "You will wash your hair every single day. Your five minutes in the shower includes washing your hair. Did you hear me, my little Prima Donnas?"

"Ma'am, yes ma'am!"

"Black girls." I didn't perk up. I wanted to shrink, run, hide. I didn't want to be singled out as being different or even the same for that matter. Especially not here, in this foreign land, surrounded by a bunch of women from all over the United States who ranged in age from seventeen (like me) to twenty-five. I wanted to blend in—be the same. Maybe that was part of why I joined the military in the first place: to feel a part of something, to feel essential, to feel as one. "You will wash your hair once a week. I understand that your hair is different and can't be washed every day or else you'll go bald. I really don't give a shit if any of you go bald. But I'd rather not hear a bunch of whining and crying about your goddamned hair so I'm granting you permission to wash your hair once a week. Is that clear?"

Frightened out of our skulls, each of us, black and white, exclaimed, "Ma'am, yes ma'am!"

Together, we would get through the next six weeks by working together, praying together, and crying together. Occasionally, in a rare moment of pleasure, we'd get to scarf down home-baked brownies someone's mother had sent in a care package. We lost a few peers along the way. Some were shipped back home with what was left of their pride.

But for the rest of us, we found a place where we belonged.

What in the hell am I doing here? The thought came to me as I sat in class listening to the banal chatter between my instructor and my classmates.

I don't belong here.

After basic training, every Airman went to Technical School to learn their trade. My trade was that of a Security Police. Most of my fellow enlistees in basic training had chosen their preferred career before enlisting. Ever indecisive, I decided to let Uncle Sam choose for me.

"I'd really recommend you choose a job," my recruiter had said after I enlisted. "There's nothing on this list that interests you?"

I studied the list that seemed to have five hundred different jobs on it. "The only thing I'd like to do is journalism, either print, radio or television," I said.

"You can't do that straight away. You have to do something else then cross-train into those fields unless you had that career before signing up, in which case, you'd have a better chance, but it still wouldn't be guaranteed."

I shrugged. "What happens if I choose nothing?"

"The military will choose for you."

"Sounds good to me."

"You'll end up being a cop or a cook."

"I like cooking."

"Part of the cooks job is to tag and bag."

"Tag and bag?"

"Dead people."

I had no idea if this was true or not. He swore he was telling the truth, but my recruiter, only about five years older than I was at the time, was an easy-going guy who liked to jest. Apparently in a jesting mood myself, I was in the mood to hedge my bets.

"I'll let the military choose for me. I tend to have a lot of luck."

"Good," Sergeant Greene said. "You'll need it."

I sat waiting for cop class to start, mindlessly twirling my newly-installed braids, as the instructor and students chattered around me. Yesterday the topic of conversation had been about the television show *Seinfeld*. I'd never watched an episode of *Seinfeld* in my life. Today, Auburn and Alabama dominated the classroom conversation. Again … um, what? I seemed to be the only person in the room unfamiliar with the college football rivals. My ignorance about television sitcoms or sports wasn't what bothered me. So what was? Why did I feel so utterly displaced in this environment to the point of feeling like a soldier dropped behind enemy lines? No one had ever said anything negative to me, and yet, I felt particularly conspicuous.

I'd like to say there was an epiphany when I realized I was the only black person in the room. That would be a lie. Surely, you know the instant you walk into a room that you are the only "one," whatever "one" you happen to be. It had never been an issue for me. In the years following, I'd use it to my advantage. From writing conferences to entrepreneurial seminars, my hand would always be the first to be raised, my question the first to be asked. I wanted my voice to be heard and was not intimidated by being the only "one" in the room. So if my race wasn't the issue, then what was it that had me feeling defensive?

"Your hair is too long."

My glazed-over eyes drifted up from the open book on my desk toward the sound of the commenter: the training instructor. The conversation around me had come to a halt. He studied me with narrowed gray eyes.

"Mine?" I asked. That was impossible. Part of the reason I fit so well in the military was because I was a stickler for following rules. My braids—cut into a bob style that stopped at my chin, was well above the bottom edge of my collar, as per regulation.

"Yes, yours," he said in a thick Alabaman accent. Staff Sgt. Quinn was a mildly attractive man, tall with a thin nose, sandy brown hair, and glasses. He also had a strong southern twang and looked like he chewed tobacco. "You need to make sure you cut it before you come back in here tomorrow."

"It might look like it's too long because I'm sitting down, but when I stand at attention—"

"Airman Eason." Staff Sgt. Quinn said, the humor in his eyes when he conversed with the other students now gone. He pushed up his round spectacles. "I have no intention of having a discussion about this. Your hair is too long. Cut it." He turned to his podium. "Now let's start class."

I was furious. I'd recently ventured off base and had my hair braided into a short bob. I was certain that my hair was within regulation. In a fit of vengeance, I raced off to the local BX and bought myself a relaxer kit. I could have just cut my braids, sealed the tips, and have been done with it. But I wanted to do something more drastic. I wanted to send Staff Sgt. Quinn a message that I knew damned well what the problem was, and it wasn't my hair being too long. It was because my hair was in braids. They were a stark reminder that I was different from the rest of the students in class.

Back in my dormitory I began to undo my braids, rage fueling my fingers. About a half an hour later, when they were all removed, I applied the relaxer to my hair. All done, I looked at myself in the mirror. I turned my head from side to side. At eighteen years old you'd think I'd know a thing or two about hair by now. I didn't. But at least my hair was straight and short and suitable for blending with the society I found myself in.

I was keenly aware that I'd just bitten off my nose to spite my face. I'd reacted to Staff Sgt. Quinn's comments rashly, in hopes of showing him a thing or two. But what was I showing him? That I'd abandon my own hairstyle, part of my own heritage to assimilate? Why did I have to be such a hothead? Why didn't I just snip a half an inch off my braids and let it be? Perhaps that's what Staff Sgt. Quinn was also thinking when he saw me the next day. He did a double take, furrowed his brows, but said nothing.

I was three months into my military career and, much like in high school, I was aching to fit in. I wanted the military to open its arms to me and be the extended family I never had. And I wasn't going to let a little thing like hair get in the middle of that. Soon, I'd be at my first Air Force Base, ready for duty, and this experience would fade away like a bad memory.

My first assignment had been High Wycombe Air Station in England. After a short sixteen-month assignment, the base was put on the closure list, and I moved on to Spangdahlem Air Force Base in Germany. In England, I wore the ubiquitous ponytail with the side part. Now, in Germany, where everything was increased tenfold—a bigger base meant more clubs, more people, more opportunities to see and be seen. At twenty, I wanted to freshen up my look, get a decent haircut, look pretty.

Perched on the bed of my dormitory, I picked up the phone to call the only salon on the base. And then I thought I'm a grown woman. An adult. I don't have to hide behind a telephone. What if they accept walk-ins? I should just go over there, walk in, and ask for a relaxer and cut.

Ah, growing up and becoming my own woman, finding my own voice felt so darned liberating!

I walked into the shop and saw the lone stylist tending to a client. The stylist was a blonde woman, which concerned me. Can white people do black people's hair? Were they familiar with the intricacies in relation to Negro hair? "Hi," I said. "How much for a relaxer and cut?"

The blonde woman smiled and said in a sweet voice, "I'm sorry, but we can't do your kind of hair here."

I stood inside the beauty salon and prayed the tiled floors would open beneath me and suck me in.

The woman must have noticed my shock because she repeated herself. "I'm sorry." She pointed around the salon, as if showing me proof. There was another woman there— also white—who busied herself by sweeping the floor. I looked back at the stylist who was dabbing hair coloring onto her client's strands then wrapping it in foil. Aluminum foil on hair? What in the world? "There's just no one on staff that can do your kind of hair."

"Okay, thanks!" I said, then jetted out of the salon.

I walked back to my dormitory and tried to put my finger on what it was that I was feeling? Was that what they called systematic racism? Was it discrimination? I'm on a military base. I'm a member of the military. But I can't walk into the salon on base and get my hair done? Were they actively soliciting for a black hairstylist (or any hairstylist) that could do black hair? Military wives who weren't in the military resided on the base. Surely, one of them was available to do hair, right? What should I do? Should I call the base commander and complain? Should I start a petition? And what in hell were all the other black women doing to maintain their hair? We were in Spangdahlem, not Atlanta. I couldn't very well go off the base and stumble into a black hair salon. Could I?

I was incensed. Embarrassed that my hair required special care that could not be easily attained on base, I went back to my room and mulled over the issue with my roommate.

"Girl, you just gotta ask somebody," Edgar, my roommate, suggested in her Georgian twang after I told her about my experience. She was lucky. She had a thick bushel of fine, water wavy hair that she could pull back in a ponytail and be done with. She didn't need a relaxer to get a comb through her hair as I did.

"Ask who?"

"Anybody you see with braids. Ask them who did it. Then go over there and get your hair done."

"Edgar, we shouldn't have to do that. The military shouldn't make us feel as though we're aliens on a military base. If white men and white women have a place to go to get their hair washed, we should too. It's the nineties for crying out loud!"

I felt as if I'd been relegated to the back of the bus by the very entity I was voluntarily serving.

Edgar shrugged as if she'd seen worse atrocities in the South in her twenty years of living, and this one didn't measure up. She was also one of those people who couldn't seem to talk without smiling. So she smiled and said, "I'll let you know if I find someone who can do braids."

Word of mouth. A simple "Your hair is nice. Who did it?" would be the method for clients and stylists alike to find a means of survival on the base. And as such, I found a braider. Linda was the wife of a military man. She wasn't all that good, and I suspect she was practicing on each client. But she lived on base, had a reasonable price, and was someone with whom you didn't mind spending four hours of your life. I sat at a dining room chair in Linda's place and let her braid my hair while we bonded over diets and remembrances of home. But even as I eased into the realization that my short-term problem was solved, I quietly worried about the next base and the next.

After all, these braids wouldn't last forever.

23

Nothing is a waste of time if you use the experience wisely.

Auguste Rodin

Beauty Be Us

Al and I met in the gym at our last assignment in Germany. I was working hard at not working up a sweat on a recumbent bike when he swaggered over to make conversation.

"Hey, you want to ride to Ramstein with me and a couple of friends?" he asked.

"Who are you?"

"They call me Big Al."

"Big Al, I don't get in cars with strangers."

"You ever been to Ramstein Air Force Base?"

"Nope," I replied. Big Al proceeded to tell me it was about ninety minutes from our base, Spangdahlem, and was much more impressive. Still, I didn't know the dude, and whereas I was impulsive about all things hair, I hit the brakes when it came to men—especially those who went by monikers like Big Al.

"What's your name?"

"Eason," I said. In the military it's easy to forget you actually have a first name. "Rhonda."

"Where you from, Eason Rhonda?"

"Detroit."

"No way. Me too."

My interest was piqued. Turned out, Al and I lived a block away from one another in Detroit. We never made that trip to Ramstein, but we stuck to each other like glue until we got new assignments later that year. He was headed to Georgia, and I was headed to Florida. We promised to continue our relationship via long distance. And since he was my first real boyfriend, I actually believed we would.

Tampa, Florida. Finally! After almost four years of serving overseas, I'd returned home to American soil. I could've kissed the ground when the double doors of Tampa International Airport opened and the ninety-degree heat and swamp-like humidity wrapped itself around me, welcoming me to my first stateside assignment. I'd arrived at midnight, and the illuminated city wowed me. Sure, I'd visited France and Italy, but there was nothing like being back in the good old U.S. of A. I was home. As much as I enjoyed my foreign travels, I was ecstatic to be back in America. And Tampa, a year-round summer playground at that. No more winter coats. No more driving on the wrong side of the road. No more judgmental looks when I asked for ketchup with my pomme frites instead of mayonnaise.

Not only had I left the overseas assignments behind, I'd also left my career as a security police officer. I'd applied and been accepted for reassignment as a paralegal. That meant I was leaving the combat boots and green battle dress uniform behind, and I'd get to wear my cute light blue blouse, my navy skirt and ... wait for it ... heels to work every day. I'd look like a proper lady as I pranced around the only office I'd ever worked in. My optimism shot through the roof.

Of course, one of the first matters of business was finding my new best friend: a hairstylist. I had never had a regular hairstylist, and now that I lived in Tampa, I could put down roots. And under the bright lights of a big city like Tampa, it would be a pinch. (Um, yeah … so … not a pinch. Not a pinch, not a cinch, not a zip, and most certainly not a snap. But my optimism was as warm and cuddly as a two-month old puppy, right?)

Finding the salon had been as simple as scrolling through the yellow pages. I let my fingers do the walking and stumbled upon one not too far from MacDill Air Force Base. I called the shop and told them to pencil me in at 11:00 AM for a relaxer and trim. The receptionist was polite and efficient and gave me little reason to believe that the act of penciling me in was simply a condition of her employment and had nothing to do with what time I'd actually get to plant my derriere in the seat. As such, on the day of my appointment, I practically skipped to my decades-old dark green Mercury Tracer and drove to my appointment with an actual paper map guiding me along the way.

I arrived in the parking lot fifteen minutes early. There was the salon, tucked inside of a strip mall in a sketchy part of town. The windows were darkened so seeing inside was impossible. I didn't need to see inside. I *knew* what was happening behind that darkened glass. Magic! Miracles! Madams of Marvelousness were transforming women from drab to fab, and I wanted in. And I had an appointment. Maybe my beautician could see me sooner than expected? Yes. Of course. It's possible that my assigned beautician— what was her name?—LaTrecia—was sitting in an empty chair, flipping through a current edition of Sophisticate's Black Hair wishing her 11 o'clock could come a little earlier so she could take an early lunch. *I will not make LaTrecia wait for me a second longer!*

I got out of the car and headed to the door. When I opened it, I thought I'd entered a building that people should've been running out of instead of walking into. Thick, gray smoke polluted the air. It took a moment for my eyes to adjust to my surroundings. When they did, I wasn't thrilled at what I saw. I'd been in black salons in Detroit before, but Charlene's was no BeautyBeUs. (And yes, the unfortunate grammatically incorrect name should have tipped me off, but no.)

There were two rows of about seven chairs. Each chair had a client in it being serviced, which affirmed my decision in choosing this salon. The fact that each chair had a client meant that this salon was the place to be. The young woman at the counter took my name, checked me off a list, and made her way to a young woman with a super short haircut, presumably to tell her I was her next client.

The stylist—who couldn't have been more than twenty-five—eyed me with suspicion, as though I weren't a stranger and prospective client, but instead a person who might have been featured on America's Most Wanted. I smiled and gave a quick wave. She turned back to the head she was styling. Alrighty, then.

I found a seat among the eight or so other clients sitting by the front window. A couple fanned themselves with magazines. Most of them slept. This was before cellphones were available to the masses. I wanted nothing to distract me from watching my new beautician perform her craft, but before I could get comfortable, the receptionist was back in front of me.

"Rhonda? Come on back and let me base your head."

Well now. This was different. Frou frou salons had wash girls. They took the menial tasks of washing, conditioning, and sometimes blow-drying the client's hair away from the stylist so the stylist could focus on more complex, talent- and education-driven tasks, thereby utilizing her skills more efficiently. The goal was less wait-time for the client and possibly a tip for the wash girl. However, this was not a frou frou salon. This salon was in the straight-up 'hood, so this forward-thinking process was quite impressive. I sat at the washbowl while the young woman opened her jar of base, which was nothing more than petroleum jelly that prevents the sodium hydroxide in the relaxer from burning the scalp. Ahh … she had nice gentle fingers. The pointy end of the plastic rattail comb felt good on my scalp as the young woman parted my hair in several sections and rubbed base into my scalp. It was a gentle process that could have taken several minutes more, and I wouldn't have minded a bit. Alas, it was over soon after it began. Off I went back to the front of the shop, stepping over outstretched feet of sleeping clients. It was a little odd to see clients sleeping in the salon *before* they got under the hair dryer, but hey, maybe they worked really, really hard during the week.

Fifteen minutes passed. I began to get antsy. I was born into this world with many admirable qualities: optimism and kindness and … well … I'm sure there are lots more I could think of if I had the time. One of the things I was not born with was patience. If patience was a muscle then I was a wimpy woman in need of a serious workout. Perhaps that's why God directed me to BeautyBeUs.

The smoke from the burning hair was thick as mucous. I watched LaTrecia work, admiring the care and attention she gave to the client's hair. Then I really *looked* at what she was doing. The client in her chair had a super short haircut. The longest part of her hair at the top was *maybe* one-half inch long. LaTrecia used small curling irons to curl each piece of itty-bitty hair sections. She had finished about one quarter of the client's hair, working from the back to the front. This was not good. This was not good at all.

The heat from the waiting bodies and curling irons and the brutal humidity that swept in from the outside with every opening of the front door converged with one another. My eyelids became heavy. I was annoyed, yes. But I was also so very tired. Maybe I could close my eyes for just a minute….

I stretched and yawned as my body slowly awakened to the sound of a favorite old-school R&B jam playing overhead. There was nothing more rejuvenating than a mid-day nap. *Wait. Where am I? I'm still here? I'm still here!* I looked at my watch. 11:45. My appointment was at 11:00. I got here at 10:45. I looked at LaTrecia to see which of the waiting clients she was working on because surely some of these women under the dryers or waiting beside me were hers, too, right? *Oh, sweet Jesus. You've got to be kidding me.* She was still putting micro curls in the same clients hair. Oh, hell no.

"Excuse me," I said to the receptionist. "You can cross me off the books for today. I'm leaving."

I didn't bother to ask how much longer. I was done.

LaTrecia overheard me and asked, "What time was your appointment supposed to be?"

What time? Didn't the receptionist tell her as soon as I walked in that I was her 11 o'clock appointment? Or was she whispering sweet nothings into her ear?

"My appointment was at 11," I said, trying to keep my cool.

LaTrecia sucked her teeth and rolled her eyes. "Oh. You weren't about to be seen no time soon."

What the hell? I stood stunned and looked around the salon. Is this how professionals handled their business? I understood that beauty salons rent out their individual booths and, as such, beauticians are really independent entrepreneurs. But does a beautician ever have such a huge book of clients and care so little for her personal reputation and that of her salon that she can be so blatantly rude to a customer? And what was the point of making an appointment if there was no intention of it being honored?

I stormed out of the salon looking every bit a crazy person with my hair—sectioned off and based with petroleum jelly—sticking straight up to the sky like tumbleweed.

At the nearest store I could find, I bought an Optimum relaxer, and drove home. Before I got in the door of my dormitory, I was already dialing Toya to tell her my story of waiting an hour to get my hair done and *still* not getting my hair done. But before I did all that, I did this:

I hopped in my car and broke down into tears right outside the shop. I wasn't angry because I didn't get my hair done. Nor was I frustrated or disappointed that I didn't get my hair done. I was downright pissed off that a young black woman who was in a position to display professionalism and courtesy had failed so miserably. That her ratchet behavior superseded her desire to be successful—to protect her reputation—which, some could argue, is the most important thing we have. I was angry that there was no manager or on-site owner who cared enough about the name on the door—such as it was—to ensure that every client left pleased and pampered as much as they could make possible.

I was angry that the stylist didn't care about her treatment of a paying (and potentially loyal) customer. I was angry that the clients who were waiting in their peaceful slumber were so accustomed to being treated like second-class citizens that it never occurred to them to expect or demand better.

And so they slept.

And I wept.

And then we all moved on with our lives.

24

Etiquette does not render you defenseless. If it did, even I wouldn't subscribe to it. But rudeness in retaliation for rudeness just doubles the amount of rudeness in the world.

Judith Martin

We Are Family

The year I moved to Tampa was 1994. It was the beginning of living the next thirteen years of my life as a minority in a predominately white, middle-class enclave. On television, the year was the beginning of shows I couldn't remotely identify with: *Friends, Party of Five,* and *My So-Called Life.* On the radio, Ace of Base dominated the airwaves with one massive hit after another. Celine Dion further cemented the power of her voice with "The Power of Love." Whether I realized it or not, pop culture wasn't exactly saturated with people who looked like me at the top of the music or movie charts. And those who did have brown skin— Salt-N-Peppa, Janet Jackson, Toni Braxton, En Vogue, Lynn Whitfield, Nia Long, et cetera—were usually rocking looks that required them to cover up their natural hair in some way: wigs, weaves, relaxers. And I was no different from them in that respect. There was no place for kinks in the kingdom of beauty. Therefore, my quest for a beautician continued.

It had been a few months after my disastrous experience at BeautyBeUs. I'd decided to venture back into the hedonistic halls of hair salons. In general, my life was as uncomplicated as it could be for a woman of any age—but at twenty-two mine was particularly uneventful. My work at the legal office at MacDill was banal and unchallenging. My shiny new boyfriend was stationed only two hundred miles away at Moody Air Force Base in Valdosta, Georgia.

I was blissfully in love with my ever-faithful boyfriend whom I saw only a couple of times per month. He assured me he was one of those rare guys who enjoyed sex once a month. How perfectly convenient was that? In my head, we would get married, raise two dogs together, travel the globe, and live happily ever after. Did I mention I was twenty-two and wonderfully naive? And I continued to pursue my bachelor's degree in the evenings at the University of Tampa. But a boring job, a celibate boyfriend, and a brutal class schedule were only footnotes to my life. My main priority was looking good. Everyone knew that when you looked good on the outside, you felt good on the inside. I wasn't obsessed with shoes or jewelry or even my weight (although I did a good job of keeping it in check). No, only one thing could make me feel good on the outside and that was achieving the beautiful mane of hair that I deserved.

The salon was in a good area of Tampa. Although it was also located in a strip mall, the exterior looked professional and welcoming. When I stepped inside I felt as though I'd entered a house party. Laughter and music emanated throughout the small salon. All eyes looked at me as the front bell hanging off the door jingled behind me. There was no receptionist to greet me. I smiled, waved, and took a seat. I wasn't bold enough to enter and state my name and business. I saw eyes dart to one another in confusion.

Finally, the stylist closest to the door reluctantly asked, "Do you have an appointment?"

"Yes," I said as friendly as I could be. "With Carla."

From the disappointed look on her face, she must have been Carla.

"Have you been here before?" she asked.

"No, first time."

"What're you getting done?"

"Deep condition and style," I said. Baby steps. This was an easy task that any beauty school student should be able to handle. No harsh chemicals. No scissors. No problem.

"I'll be with you in a moment."

She wasn't blatantly rude nor overly polite. As far as I was concerned, she was still in the running to be my new best friend, my confidant, my personal miracle worker. Carla continued on with her beauty shop conversation. Everyone in the shop seemed to be in on it.

As I continued to sit, I felt woefully out of place. The front area where I sat had a high reception desk that partially obscured my view to the rest of the shop. So even if I wanted to chime in, I couldn't. I felt as though I had been invited to a party, but I didn't know any of the guests. And no one bothered to introduce me.

That's okay. That's fine. I'm a loner by nature. I *enjoy* being alone.

"Come on."

A young, thin sista who looked like she was still in high school stood before me with a look on her face that said she wanted to be anywhere other than there. I'd seen her in the shop when I'd first arrived, sweeping the hair on the floor with all the energy of a tortoise. She set the broom aside and escorted me to a washbowl.

Seriously. I decided that I hated the multiple-people-styling-my-hair-bullshit. I felt that BeautyBeUs had teased me, pulled a bait-and-switch and left me running out of the place crushed by a dismal lack of respect for Father Time.

I followed the girl to the washbowl. I sat in the seat while she attempted first-degree manslaughter by strangulation as she snapped the apron around my neck. I leaned back in the seat, tilted my neck back so that it fit snuggly into the depression of the washbowl. Shampoo girl turned on the water.

"Ouch! Can you make that warmer?" I asked.

It was customary—or so I thought—for a stylist to adjust the water temperature and pressure in the bowl before applying it to the client's hair. But hey, what do I know? More than she does, I thought, remembering that Shampoo Girl doubled as the cleaning lady and may have been none-too-thrilled about one (or both) of her duties.

I flinched again as scalding hot water burned my scalp. I jumped. She sucked her teeth and adjusted the temperature again. She did not, I noticed, adjust the pressure of the water. It gushed out of the handle like water from a garden hose set on full blast. This chick was seriously pissing me off.

She lathered up my hair—scrub, scrub—then rinsed out the shampoo.

What the—? Was that it?

She did it again. Lather—scrub, scrub—rinse.

Not my style of hair washing but okay, I'll roll with it.

Try not to be a bitch, Rhonda. Nobody likes a bitch, Rhonda.

Laughter continued to fill the shop. No one was supervising the Shampoo Girl who was doing a lousy job at impressing me with her customer service skills.

In all my travels I had never felt so disconnected and unwelcome than in this black salon surrounded by my own people.

The droplets began.

As I lay with my head back, seeing little more than the peeling ceiling above me, speckles of water began to dot my face. *No big deal.* There's always a little water that splashes on the face.

Then more droplets of water.

I closed my eyes.

And then more.

My temperature rose to match that of the water dousing my face.

"Stop. Stop. Never mind!" I said.

Shampoo Girl stood back, hand on her hip, her posture begging the question, *So what you gonna do about it?*

What I wanted to do was get up and sock her one. But I didn't do that for several reasons. First: I'm a pacifist. Socking people just because I wanted to wasn't my bag. Second: it was clear that this group of people in the shop were a family—an extended family, perhaps—but a family nonetheless. I was not family. I was a stranger, an X factor who'd stumbled into their private enclave. This was not the place to start asserting aggressive behavior, even if it was in my personality to do so—and it wasn't.

I got up out of my seat, with a sopping wet head.

"I'll have to come back another day," I said, yanking the apron from around my neck.

"What happened?" Carla asked. She was putting the finishing touches on her client's hair.

I didn't answer. I didn't need too. I'd never see any of these people again. I clutched my purse and stormed out of

209

the virtual house party that didn't seem to need nor want my patronage.

"I hate unprofessional black people!" I yelled through the phone to my sister when I'd gotten home. "Why are we so shiftless?"

Oh, God how I vented!

"Yeah," she said, nonplussed by my vile language. "That's why when you get one who's halfway decent, you stick with her for life. Good, professional hairstylists are hard to find, girl. Especially if they're black. When you get one you like, you better hold onto her like she's a lifeboat on the Titanic."

Of course, not *all* black people were unprofessional when it came to minding their business. There were some out there who took their work, their reputation, and customer service very seriously.

My permanent stylist in Tampa would teach me that sometimes a girl had to kiss a few frogs to find a princess. And it would be worth the wait. But before I met her, I'd kiss a couple more slimy frogs.

25

If it sounds too good to be true, it is.

Anonymous

The Red-Headed Weaver

I was itching for some fake hair. If I could get a good sew-in weave to cover up my own hair, then I wouldn't have to stress about getting my hair done so often. And I wanted *hair* not braids. (Weaves and extensions are often used interchangeably. Weaving—the method of sewing wefts of human or synthetic hair onto hair that has been cornrowed—is a type of extension process.) I drove around Tampa but was skeptical about going into any old place that had We Do Weaves in the window. One day, by happenstance, I saw an advertisement in a newspaper. A full-service salon that installed the most advanced weaves. Did I deserve the most advanced weave? Yes, yes I did. I called the shop from work.

"Do you do black hair?" I asked without hesitation.

What sounded like a Caucasian woman who'd inhaled one too many Virginia Slims, said, "Yes, oh my, darling, we do all types of hair."

"I want to get a weave done. How much do you charge?"

"We'd have to see your head but it might be, oh, a hundred, maybe one fifty. Let me make you an appointment."

She's eager. Good sign.

"Where exactly are you located? I'd like to drop in for a consultation first."

"Fine, fine. But it's easier if I just give you an appointment. You'll be beautiful. We do beautiful extensions here."

"Your exaction location?" I asked, still getting used to finding my way around Tampa.

She gave me her cross streets, and I promised her I'd swing by that evening after work.

"Who should I ask for?"

"I'll be here, darling. My name is Red."

In a world without GPS, finding Red's shop proved daunting. After lots of driving and U-turns, I finally figured out that her shop was tucked away in a strip mall (yet *another* strip mall.) There was no name on the door, just an address. When I stepped inside, my heart stopped. I thought I'd found my way into a hoarder's house.

There were mannequin heads for wigs everywhere. Beauty supplies—opened and used— were lying about. There was no real order to the place. It was as if I'd stepped inside of someone's crowded basement, or an old hair museum. It had no resemblance to a hair salon *at all.*

"I'm here, darling. I was expecting you."

Red came out from behind a curtain that separated that disastrous front area from the back. Looking at her made me want to run back out the door. I was desperate for a weave. But was I *that* desperate? She had on a terrible red wig that was matted in clumps (*how is that even possible?*) and askew. Thick black eyeliner looked as if it had been applied by a member of Kiss. Her leathery skin was brown from too much tanning. She wore green eye shadow and red lipstick, and she looked as if she wouldn't have been the least bit surprised if I had told her something was crawling on her freckled arm. Nothing was, but it *could* have been.

"Red," she said and extended her hand. "Lovely to meet you."

Why even bother? Why not turn around, say you got the wrong place, and leave?

"Nice to meet you, Red." Let's make this quick. "You do weaves, right?"

"Yes, darling. Lots of hair extensions. We've had movie stars in here. I'm the best. I was one of the first in this area to do extensions."

I didn't know much about weaves, but I did know that the kind I wanted would require that my own hair be braided. I found it hard to believe that this woman, who was now coughing up a lung, knew how to wash black hair, much less braid it.

"What method do you use?" I asked more out of curiosity than genuine interest. A cat hissed behind the curtain. *Oh, Lord.*

"Glue. It's the best kind. You can't even tell you've got the extensions in."

I looked around the shop as she continued to talk. There were tightly curled white wigs on Styrofoam mannequin heads. Green and purple wigs that looked Halloween-ready hung from a wall as if Red could pluck one up and put it on her own head at a moment's notice. My eyes stopped on a droplet of something on the shag carpet. Was that cat dropping? *No, Rhonda. Cats use a litter box.* So if that didn't come from a cat, what did it come from?

"Come, darling. Do you want me to start on your hair? I can make you look beautiful. One ten for you since you're in the military," she said, noting my Air Force Blues. "That's the best price."

"You know, Red. I think I need to give it a bit more thought."

I was ready to leave. I felt like I was in a Stephen King novel. There was no window looking out of the salon, and I was afraid that I could seriously go missing in that dungeon.

"Come back then. Think about it and come back. Red's always here."

"Thanks, Red."

I ran out of that place wondering how many more hellholes my quest for beautiful hair was going to lead me before I finally got what I wanted.

26

Ask the experienced rather than the learned.
Arabic proverb

An Expensive Lesson

I had a kinship with substance abusers. I've never been an addict, but in my mind I feel that I could identify with the urges alcoholics got when they ached for a mid-morning sippy sip. Or the feeling a heroin addict got when it was time for another hit. Logic and rationale abandoned me when I felt the need to change my hair. The antsy anticipation of change consumed my waking thoughts. I noticed, analyzed, approved, or rejected the hairstyle of every woman I encountered, black or white. With the advent of hair extensions, there was literally *no* hairstyle I could not have. I would pour over *Hype Hair* or *Sophisticates' Black Hair* magazines in the hopes of finding a hairstyle that expressed who I was in that moment.

I was a woman obsessed. It was as though changing my hair would change my circumstances.

Hate my job?

Get a new hairstyle!

Frustrated with my boyfriend?

Get a new hairstyle!

Ma's being annoying again?

Still obsessing over the guy who got away?

Irritated by the guy who won't go away?

Get a new hairstyle!

These weren't obvious questions I asked myself. My motivation was buried deep in my subconscious. On the surface, I believed that I was changing my hair for no other reason than because it was fun.

There was no denying that the entire salon experience— when it was a good one—from smelling the fragrant shampoo, feeling strong fingers massage my scalp, reveling beneath the sharp nails that dug into my scalp, dozing soundly under a hooded dryer, staring into the mirror as I transformed into that-girl-with-the-beautiful-hair, and strutting out of the salon and into the world with my new hairdo, new perspective, and new attitude—shot my dopamine levels sky high making me drunk with happiness. And who doesn't enjoy being drunk with happiness?

I'd driven by the upscale salon many times. Curiosity propelled me to go inside and check things out. I still didn't have a permanent beautician and survived by putting in my own relaxers. It had been a long time since I'd had a "salon high."

The inside of the salon was, indeed, elegant and professional. I spotted only one black hairstylist in the salon who happened to be sitting in her own chair thumbing through a magazine. I asked the polite receptionist if they do weaves. I'd never had a weave put in my head, and I couldn't stand seeing another photo of Naomi Campbell or Janet Jackson and not knowing what it was like to be able to toss long hair around without risk of a strong Florida wind blowing it clear across the Tampa Bay.

"Yes, we do," she said. "Let me get Janine to talk to you."

The receptionist went and spoke to the black stylist who offered me a polite smile and came up front to chat.

"Janine," she said, extending a manicured hand out to me. She was tall, dark, and looked capable enough. One could never judge hairstylists on anything other than their work. Looking at them—even their hair—was no indication at all of what they could do. My two favorite stylists always had messy, unkempt hair. Hairstylists were not always walking billboards of their talent. "How can I help you?"

"Hi, I'm Rhonda," I said. "Do you do weaves?"

"I do" she replied.

There was something very officious about her, not overly friendly, not rude, but business-like.

"Good," I said. This was an auspicious start. I hadn't really prepared a list of questions to pose to my new transformer. As far as I was concerned she was black and could do weaves, a relatively new creation available at reasonable prices for the masses. What more did I need to know?

"What kind?" I probed, like the good journalism reporter I studied in night school to become. "Glue-in, sew-in, bonding? I hear Janet Jackson gets bonding."

"I do sew-ins. It's the safest method for the hair. Have you ever had extensions before?"

"No," I said.

Janine explained, "Your hair will be braided into cornrows. Wefts of weave are then sewn onto the tracks of the cornrows, cut and styled. I can give you a partial weave—which means some of your own hair around the top and around the edges stays out and relaxed to blend naturally with the weave, or we can braid your entire head and sew in the weave."

"Cool," I replied, knowing that Janine was already hired. However, I still had another question to ask. This was little more than checking boxes at this point. "How much do you charge?"

"Three hundred dollars."

Wh— wha— what? Surely, I'd misheard her.

"How much?"

"Three hundred."

I didn't have three hundred dollars. I had about negative two hundred dollars in my checking account, but I was sure that wouldn't help. I had to figure out a way to get this done, and to justify the expense.

"How long does it last?"

Janine shrugged. "Depends on how well you take care of it."

What kind of answer was that? Did that mean a year if I treated it like freshly spooled silk?

"On average," I pressed.

"Three months," she said.

Three months. This style would average a hundred bucks a month. I calculated in my head: two professional relaxers in three months would be about $120; two self-applied relaxers in a three-month span would cost about twenty bucks.

I sighed. I had to figure this out. The issue wasn't *if* I was going to get the weave installed, it was *how* and *when.* I looked at Janine who hadn't flinched when she quoted her price. She was very confident in herself. Her no-haggle stance made me even more certain that she was a weave master that I had to use. Even so, my annoying gut told me to leave, think about it, at the very least, ask more questions.

"Do you have a picture book of clients with weaves you've installed before?" Great question, Rhonda! Look at her previous work *before* making the decision to pay her such an extravagant amount of money.

"No," she said. "I've done this for years, but no, I don't have a book."

My joy dipped quickly, as if I were on a jolting carnival ride.

Janine must have sensed my indecision because she said, "By the way, that amount includes the hair."

Well now we're talking! Good quality hair alone could cost $300. This really was a bargain after all. I knew it. Why would God lead me into this salon with four inches of hair if he didn't want me to walk out with twelve inches of hair?

"When can I get an appointment?"

Janine smiled. "I'll check my book." She went back to her chair and returned with a piece of paper and an appointment book. "Next Saturday is good for you?"

"Yes," I said. How was my anxious self going to make it to next Saturday? I felt like a child on Christmas Eve. Imagine experiencing that night-before-Christmas feeling for seven days. A person could burst open from the anticipation.

"Eleven o'clock good? It'll take me three hours at the most."

"Perfect," I replied.

Janine jotted my name down in her book.

"I'll need a major credit card and your signature on here," she said, handing me a piece of paper with a carbon duplicate.

Credit card? Signature? I'm in a hair salon not a car dealership.

"What's this?" I stuttered. At the top of the form were eight letters I understood perfectly well. CONTRACT.

"It says that if you're more than fifteen minutes late for your appointment you'll be charged an additional $25. The $150 deposit you'll give me today will be non-refundable, even if you're a no-show. When your hair is done, you'll just owe the balance of one-fifty."

My eyes scanned the page. The contract also said that I could not sue her or the salon for money in any amount if I was unhappy with my hair for any reason. Sue her? Did people sue their salons or stylists? I didn't even know such a thing existed. And why would anyone do that? People were stupid.

I ignored the part of my brain that, at this point, was screaming for me to leave, think about it, reconsider. I signed my name with a flourish and dug in my wallet for a Visa card that may or may not have had three hundred dollars credit available on it. Janine swiped the card. We both watched the machine and waited for its slow reply. I released my clenched cheeks when the machine sputtered out a receipt.

"Here you are, Rhonda."

"Janine, I look forward to seeing you next Saturday!"

I floated out of the salon wondering if a fool had just parted with her money….

"I think I like it," I said to myself as I studied my image in my dorm room mirror. I turned my hair this way and that. "I do like it. It's cute."

If I said those words enough, maybe they would start to sound like the truth.

Janine had indeed installed a weave. A $300 weave. As it was my first weave ever, I had nothing to compare it to. It was a thick mass on my head that stopped just below my shoulders and curled under. The too-long bangs were curled with a wide-barreled hot iron. My hair looked circa the early eighties when it was all about volume. I had no choice but to like it; I'd paid for it. It had to last me three months.

I raked my fingers through my hair and looked at my hand. Was my hair supposed to shed like this? I let the wisps of hair float into the garbage can. Okay, fine. I just won't touch it. I smiled, pouted, vogued at my reflection. I swung the hair that eight-year-old me would not have believed could be true. Then I looked at the wisps of hair floating to the floor. Okay, so … I won't swing my hair either. Don't touch. Don't swing.

I pranced into my workplace, the base legal office, and answered all of the questions I knew were coming.

"No, I didn't cut my hair."

"You're right, there is something different about me."

"No, it's not a wig."

"Nope, didn't cut my hair."

"A weave."

"They sewed a weft of hair into my scalp. Yep, through the skin and all. Nope, didn't hurt a bit." (Yes, mischievous me *actually* told someone that, and yes, they *actually* believed it.)

"It didn't cost much." To Joan Collins it didn't cost much!

There was no way I could focus on work that week. In fact, I wished I didn't have to leave my chair. Not because of the people and their questions but because of the hair itself. It caused me far too much anxiety to keep looking on the floor behind me, at the trail of hair that I left in my wake. I was a squirrel running away with more nuts than I could carry. It was everything I could do not to pick up the strands, which seemed to be coming out in greater quantities as I walked down the hall. I had to remind myself not to touch my hair in meetings because I'd only be pulling out strands of hair. Sometimes, if I breathed too heavily, hair would fall from my head, drift in front of my eyes like a leaf on a cool fall day, and land on my lap.

I officially felt foolish.

I tried bundling the hair up into a ponytail. A rubber band could barely contain the thick mass sprouting from my head.

I officially looked foolish.

The weave lasted one week. It was all the mortification I could take. After I told Toya about it, I called my father some days later, still miffed over the money I'd lost.

"How much did you pay?" he asked although I'd already told him.

"Three hundred dollars."

"Oh my. That's a lot of money for hair."

Hell, that was a lot of money for *food.*

"I know. I want to sue her, but she made me sign a contract."

"Read me the contract," he said.

I did. My father, the newspaper editor, chuckled. "Well, it sounds like she was sick and tired of having people drag her into court for doing a lousy job on their hair so she protected herself. I guess you'll have to chalk it up to a

three hundred dollar lesson. Let's hope your next lesson
will be cheaper."

27

Luck is not chance, it's toil; fortune's expensive smile is earned.

Emily Dickinson

My Lucky Penney

There were lots of great ways to temporarily cure anxiety. Sex was one, but my beloved was a million miles away so he was useless. Food was another. However, I spent a lot of time in the gym and wasn't interested in eating my emotions and busting out of my size six jeans. Drinking. Even though I was in my early twenties, I hadn't yet acquired the taste for alcohol. Shopping was another anxiety buster. There was no downfall to shopping as far as I could tell. And a girl always needed a new pair of jeans or tube of lipstick. Not to mention that I was a single, independent airman making at least twenty-one grand a year who'd somehow acquired a shiny new credit card.

It was on one of those anxiety relief missions to the mall that I'd stumbled by a hair salon I'd never considered before. I'd been on my way out of the shopping center, with my Rave and Wet Seal bags swinging from my arm. I'd parked somewhere around JCPenney. I headed down the escalator and circled the store, getting more lost and disoriented. That's when I smelled it. The fragrant perfume of the shampoo was unmistakable. I could identify Mizani products if I were blindfolded and set adrift at sea. Curious, I stepped inside the salon.

"Hi, sweetie. Can I help you?" A perky brunette not much older than me, batted her thickly mascara'd eyelashes.

"I'm just looking," I said, and gazed out over the brightly lit salon as though I were in a zoo instead of a hair salon.

"Sure, thing. Let me know if there's anything I can help you with."

I stood at the front of the shop, in awe of what I saw. Black and white hairstylists, men and women, worked side by side on clients of every hue. The modern-looking salon had prices printed clearly on a large menu displayed on the wall. This was an anomaly. From that day to this, I've never been in a black salon where prices were clearly written on a menu. There was minimal chatter and maximum efficiency as the salon buzzed with worker bees blow-drying, curling, and cutting as if their lives depended on it. Sure, one could argue they had all the enthusiasm of a Stepford Wife, but what I saw was corporate America's professionalism on display and customer service in motion.

This was it. I had found my place, my people, my ... huh? Those were *not* my prices.

I looked at the service menu behind the receptionist's head and analyzed the prices. Are they out of their freaking minds? Since when was JCPenney salon a place for the super-rich? By the time I got a relaxer, trim, and rinse (yes, even in my early twenties I was covering my gray) I'd be out eighty bucks! That was the difference between a frou frou salon and a 'hood salon. The neighborhood salon would offer the relaxer, trim, and rinse for sixty bucks. Year, after year, after year. Then again, the neighborhood salon would also make you wait half an hour before you were invited to sit in the chair. If ever there was something worth making a financial sacrifice for, my hair was that thing. And it wasn't like the tops in my bag, which were faddish rags that would be tossed next summer. My hair was an investment. I was anxious to grow long hair. That couldn't happen without first getting an expert to tend to my precious locks.

"Still looking?" the receptionist asked with a smile. Yep, definitely a Stepford Wife.

"I'd like to make an appointment."

"Okay, which stylist would you like, sweetie? I'll pull up her calendar."

I looked around the shop. There were at least three black women on the floor doing hair. That didn't include any who might have been off that day. Looking at the beauticians and their clients in mid-style didn't do much in the way of helping me decide who my next stylist should be.

"Um, I don't know. I've never been here before." Are you going to ask this next question face-to-face? Why, yes. Yes I am. "Can you recommend a black hairstylist for me?"

"Yes!" she said without batting a lash. "Let's see. I think you'll really like Abby. She's one of my favorites, and customers seem to always be pleased with her."

"Where is she?" I asked and turned back to the salon.

"Oh, she just went in the back to the washbowls. What day would you like to come in, and what would you like to have done?"

I looked back up at the prices. About all I could afford was a wash. Not a wash and blow-dry or set. Just a wash.

"A relaxer and rinse, please." This one would be on Visa. "Next Saturday."

The receptionist added my appointment to the computer—a computerized system!—and gave me a small reminder card with my appointment time on it. This was otherworldly shit. But I wouldn't be prematurely impressed. I would withhold my touchdown dance until after I walked out of here a satisfied customer.

The following weekend I was back at JCPenney. Abby had come to get me within moments of my arrival. She was a tall woman in her mid-to-late thirties, thin, and what the African American community would call redbone. She greeted me with a warm smile and started my services almost immediately.

Going to the stylist for the first time was kinda like going on a blind date. You hoped there would be a connection. A mutual adoration. As it happened, our conversation came easy for us, and we found we were like-minded, forward-thinking people.

After that first visit, I'd started going to Abby on a regular basis. She had been a gift from God. She wasn't interested in hairstyles as much as she was interested in hair health. That was her focus. Styles and length were secondary to health. She'd put me on a ritual of deep conditioners and often times gave me trims without charging me JCPenney's exorbitant prices. She was a business-minded person looking to expand her personal book of business. Abby got it. She was a true professional. And for that, I was happy I'd found her.

During my second or third visit, Abby finally asked me the inevitable. "Who's been doing your hair?" she asked me.

Here is a good time to pause and mention that every stylist I've ever visited for the first time—past, present and probably future—has always asked me: *Who's been doing your hair?* Or some version of it, like:

Who cut your hair?

Who colored your hair?

Who is the person that mucked your hair up this bad and forced you to walk around planet Earth like this?

233

It's almost as if every stylist knows every other stylist in their town and wants to know who's responsible for the poor excuse of a hairstyle on my head. No matter how on-point my hair was, no matter my response to the question, the follow-up response to my reply has always been: *Hmph! She doesn't know how to* _____ [Fill in the blank.]

I always wondered if this was a sales technique taught in salon schools across the country to make the client feel as though they had finally sat in the right chair. They had finally found *the one.*

"No one in particular," I replied. Which was true. Nevertheless, I'd been to enough hairdressers at this point to know what was coming.

"Um," Abby said. "Whoever did it last doesn't know how to cut."

The bravado didn't bother me. Time would tell if her work could measure up to her confidence.

After a little more conversation, Abby said in a low tone, "I gotta get out of here."

"And go where?"

"I want to own my own shop."

This was not welcome news. I didn't want her to own her own shop. I was seen in a timely manner, was treated with professionalism, and was out of that shop promptly within two hours of arriving, and I had every reason to believe it was because Big Brother was watching and didn't play no mess. If Abby branched out on her own, I feared the quality of service I'd enjoyed with her over the past few weeks would deteriorate.

"Why, this place is great, isn't it?"

"It's okay. We get benefits and steady pay, which is cool. It's the atmosphere."

"Oh, like high school, huh?"

"Worse. Always gossiping and trying to start something. I just want to work with my clients, make them look good, and go home."

"Is there tension?" I asked referring to the diversity of the shop. "Between the black and white stylists, I mean?"

"Girl, it's not the white stylists I have a problem with." She looked at me conspiratorially. "You know how we are."

"You know, Rhonda," she said as she flat-ironed my lovely hair. "It's a shame that I get along better with the white folks around here than the black. I've been dealing with this bullshit since I was a kid."

"What bullshit?" I asked.

Abby looked at me in the mirror as if I should've known what the issue was. I had no idea. Then she lightly touched a finger to the back of her hand. Ah! The universal symbol to reference skin color. Skin color was not something I'd ever had issues with so her experience as a black woman in America didn't even occur to me. Abby was a light-skinned black woman with brown freckles that dotted her nose and cheeks, and auburn-colored hair. And the woman was truly gifted when it came to hair. I could imagine the jealousy her loyal customer base caused.

I looked around the shop. The few other black women who were there that particular day were dark-skinned black women. I consider myself to be a dark-skinned black woman, and the idea of having issues with someone over light skin was stupid to me. I always liked my brown skin and preferred my men that way, too.

"I'm going to get away from them, you watch," she said with such determination I knew that it was true. "I'm going to open my own shop. One day you'll walk in here, and I'll be giving you my new address. I like you," she said. "I want you to come with me. I'm not keeping all my clients here. They'll have to hunt me down."

Abby sprayed my hair with oil spray, stood back and said, "Your hair looks great."

It wasn't a question, and it wasn't up for debate. I couldn't argue if I wanted to. I did look great.

The next time I saw Abby, I handed her a tip, and she handed me a slip of paper. On it was the new address to her very own shop. I was happy that her entrepreneurial spirit had brought her dream to fruition, while simultaneously trepidatious about what my experience in a non-corporate-managed salon would mean for me.

Only time would tell.

28

To reach something good it is very useful to have gone astray, and thus acquire experience.
Saint Teresa of Avila

Cheater

Abby had a strong, willful personality. I tended to resist those types as they reminded me too much of my mother. But Abby had been asking to read something I'd written, and I could not resist her. I'd told her I'd recently finished the first draft of my first manuscript and was anxious for feedback. (Dear Reader: Don't ever ask to read the first draft of the first manuscript of a first-time writer. Just don't. You deserve better than that kind of punishment.) Nevertheless, Abby smiled broadly as I placed my two-hundred page magnum opus titled *Secretary's Day* in her hand.

"I'm gonna read it," she promised.

Because I was a novice writer, I believed her. I was too naïve to know that people accepted manuscripts as they do Christmas cards from certain co-workers—they smile graciously when they receive them, then immediately look for the nearest trash bin.

Nevertheless, I appreciated the goodwill.

But nothing good lasts forever. My relationship with Abby endured for almost ten years, nearly the entire time I lived in Tampa. Over the course of our relationship, we were like any other couple: we had our ups and downs. The things I'd feared would happen with Abby running her own shop (coming to work late, wasting time instead of doing my hair, smoking *inside* the salon, overbooking clients thereby extending my visit by hours) never materialized. She managed her business as if she had Big Brother looking over her shoulder. It was a comfortable relationship.

But here's the thing about me: I'm not comfortable with comfort. I get antsy in relationships when things are sailing too smoothly. I need rough seas. Maybe I was looking for a reason to cheat on her. Maybe I felt she was taking my patronage for granted. Either way, she'd made a comment one too many times that eventually sent me into the arms of other lovers of hair.

"You know," she said as she put the finishing touches on my hair. "You really need to switch it up."

It was a refrain she'd been making too often lately. In fact, she was becoming relentless about wanting to change my hair.

"I like my hair like this," I said.

As much as I loved hair, I was in my Jessica-Savitch-professional-anchorwoman mode, and I didn't want anyone tinkering with perfection. For the first time in a long time, I was content. My job was okay. I was still in the Air Force, but I was making moves to separate. I was dating other guys because—let's face it—long distance romances work better in movies than real life. My hair was healthy and swinging at shoulder-length level. Why tinker with perfection?

"I'm a creative person," she said, pleading her case. "There's a lot I can do, and I want to use my skills."

I dug in my heels. "I'm the client who likes to keep the style that works for her. You have lots of clients to be creative on."

"You'd look nice with a Halle Berry cut."

"You think?"

"I know. You've got the right face and the right shape of head."

"I had my hair cut short before. It was a disaster."

"I didn't cut it."

"I'm not cutting my hair. I can't even imagine."

"It'll be easier to maintain."

"Nope."

Abby shut down the conversation before it completely went south. But as far as I was concerned, the damage was done. I'd been faithful to Abby for years, but maybe she assumed I'd never go anywhere else because she was the best stylist ever.

I'd show her.

I went back to JCPenney's. I sat in the chair of another stylist and let her wash and set my hair every so often. I hoped that my boycott of Abby's shop was making her cry buckets of tears. (Did I mention I'm a Scorpio?) I freely admit that I was feeling vengeful. I felt bullied into changing my style when I didn't want to do it. Chances are, though, Abby *wasn't* crying buckets of tears. What could I do to agitate her as much as her perceived bullying agitated me?

Something she'd said gnawed at me. That thing about looking good with the Halle Berry cut. As much as I was afraid of having someone do a whack job on my hair again, I knew beyond a doubt that Abby was gifted with the scissors. I had, after all, seen her other clients.

"Do you know how to cut hair well?" I asked the beautician applying relaxer to my hair.

"Um hmm," the woman said. She was an older woman, in her fifties. "I do good hair. Always have. I'm the best in this place."

I thought back to Abby complaining about how the black women in the shop treated her. Was this woman one of them?

"I'm thinking about getting a Halle Berry cut." That is, if I were brave enough. Imagine going back to Abby with the cut she wanted to give me? Ha! Don't pressure me and don't take me for granted, Tootsie!

"I can do that. That's easy. Shoot. You know that local news anchor Denise White?"

"I do know her," I said excitedly. "I intern at her station, and I've met her."

"I do her hair."

This was a revelation. It didn't seem all that plausible to me; yet, who would lie about something like that? Especially when I *just* said I'm an intern at her station. Which was true.

"Really?" I said. "Huh."

"Yep. I don't do her hair in the shop though. I go to her house and do it. Um hmm."

"Nice," I said, though still not quite believing. "I'll be sure to mention you the next time I see her."

Here, lady. Here is your chance to recant your story. But she didn't. So then, it must be true, right?

"You want me to cut your hair?"

I looked in the mirror and made a decision. "Yes, yes I do."

From: Rhonda Eason

To: Denise White

Subject: Your Hairstylist

Hi Denise,

I'm not sure if you remember me, but I currently intern at your station. The purpose of this email is to ask if Diane Johnson, a hairstylist at JCPenney, currently does your hair. I ask because she says she goes to your home and styles you. I'm just checking references.

Thanks again for your time.

Rhonda Eason

* * *

From: Denise White
To: Rhonda Eason

RE: Subject: Your Hairstylist

Hi Rhonda,

Thanks for reaching out. No, I'm sorry. I don't know Diane Johnson. I get that a lot though. Stylists I've never heard of stating they do my hair.

Good luck.

Denise

Ain't that about nothing? Why hadn't I emailed the anchor *before* I let that delusional woman start touching my head? It astonished me that I could be impulsive and irrational when it came to hair but smart when it came to other areas of my life.

The idea that someone would lie so blatantly was shocking to me. I wanted to go back up there and revel in the moment when I tell her I knew she was a liar. But it didn't matter. She cut my hair, and it was not a disaster. The high school haircut was a disaster. This haircut was just ... meh.

Truth be told, I missed Abby. My relationship with a stylist is a familiar one. It is a business relationship first and foremost. I pay her money, and she makes me look good, thereby making me feel good. But the lines get blurred because Abby was also my friend, my confidante, my advisor. My beauticians (I've only had two permanent beauticians in my life, and Abby was my first) are the people I can't wait to talk to when there is family drama or relationship issues. Yet, there's also a fine line in the relationship that shouldn't be crossed. As a customer, I don't want my beautician sitting eating a burger during my appointment time forcing me to wait until she finishes before I can get my hair done because she's assumed her girlfriend (me) is there just to socialize. I've put pressure on myself to keep the professional relationship intact. I wouldn't want my girlfriend pressuring me into doing something I didn't want to do, and that would include my beautician. But it was time to head back to Abby. I couldn't stay away from her another minute.

I strode into Abby's salon at once excited to be back in her place and anxious to get her opinion of my hair.

She ran her fingers through my hair, "You finally cut it."

"Yep, I need a deep condition, please."

"Who did this?"

"Um, a lady at JCPenney."

"Who?"

Oh, right. She knew them all.

"Diane?"

"She doesn't know how to cut, Rhonda. If you were going to have someone other than me cut your hair you should've at least gotten someone who can cut. Come to the washbowl."

So much for her opinion. Abby was cool but downright arrogant when it came to her skills. She knew it too and didn't apologize for it. Personally, I thought my cut looked pretty damned good. It was far from the disaster I'd gotten years earlier. Abby began to style my hair with unmasked frustration.

Finally, she blurted out, "Do you want me to fix this?"

"You have to cut it some more?"

"Yes," she said without apology. "It's uneven."

I didn't want her to cut my hair. It was short enough.

"Will you please trust me?" she said.

"Okay," I said, relenting.

I wanted to close my eyes while she butchered my hair. I had *very* little hair to cut, but Abby took what felt like fifteen minutes recutting my hair. When she was done, she said, "There. All better."

I couldn't tell. Looked almost the same to me, only shorter.

And then she curled it.

When she was done with me, I looked in the mirror in pure astonishment. I had never looked so good in my life. The cut was amazing.

Damn her. Damn Abby and her pushiness and her cockiness!

"It's hot," I said.

"I know," she said and smiled her big toothy grin. "See you in two weeks?"

I sighed, feeling properly chastised. "Yep."

29

To improve is to change; to be perfect is to change often.
Winston Churchill

All Dressed Up, Nowhere to Go

I had succumbed to Abby's pressure to change it up. She had been riding me hard about finger waves. Why? I had no idea. Maybe there had been a resurgence during the late nineties, but when I thought of finger waves I thought of 1920s glamour, not hop out of bed and wear to work every day. One day, I relented. Finger waves. They were pretty. I guess.

The looks I received when I walked into the law office—my hair a hardened helmet of tiny gelled waves that made me look more like Jermaine Jackson than Josephine Baker—was one of pure bewilderment. It was the kind of look you gave gorillas in zoos when they started making out in front of you.

And then there was the fancy ponytail. I don't know, maybe Abby had excess jars of hair gel that she was trying to get rid of. My hair was stuck up in a high, fancy ponytail that prompted the boss in the office, the Staff Judge Advocate, to ask me, "You hair looks nice. You must be going somewhere really fancy this evening. Where are you headed?"

That had been a light bulb moment for me. Where was I headed?

The moment reminded me of the movie *I'm Gonna Git You Sucka* when Flyguy gets released from prison. After more than a decade behind bars, he comes out of prison (in the eighties) wearing the very sharp duds he was locked up wearing back in the seventies. Cue music as Flyguy struts out of the jail with the misguided impression that he, the super-fly pimp, was dressed to the nines. He strutted down the street wearing a wide-brimmed yellow hat with zebra fur trim, a matching egg-yolk colored bell-bottom suit, and high-heeled fishbowl shoes—with real fish swimming in the transparent heels. When he is taunted and belittled by passersby, the truth slowly begins to dawn on him. Times have changed. He is behind the fashion curve. A relic of the past as the bevy of laughing, pointing, mocking critics have made clear. He was a mockery when—in his head—he was the fly guy.

Sigh. I didn't want to be Flyguy.

Years later I'd have a similar light bulb moment when someone explained to me that there were perfumes for all seasons. I'd had no idea, and at that time I was almost thirty years old. I loved *Red* by Giorgio Beverly Hills and wore it all year round (including riding around in the cop car when I was a Security Police Officer) when I was eighteen (yeah, probably not quite the scent for an eighteen year old either). I'd never thought that different perfumes were appropriate based on something other than desire. Society had rules I didn't even know about! For some women, they'd say to hell with society and its rules and I'll wear what I want, when I want. But I was a girl who followed the rules. I *liked* rules. Rules meant order and what kind of society would we be if people broke rules: like wearing fancy updos to work Monday through Friday or wearing a winter perfume in summer or socks with sandals. Armageddon would ensue.

I didn't want to be Flyguy.

I feared being Flyguy.

God, please don't ever let me be *that* guy.

30

You must take personal responsibility. You cannot change the circumstances, the seasons, or the wind, but you can change yourself. That is something you have charge of.

Jim Rohn

I'm Golden

I was starting to feel antsy about my own look, which I felt had become predictable and boring. It was time for a change. A major overhaul. I would not entrust this major overhaul to my number one stylist because, as my grandmother used to say, that sounded too much like right. Perhaps Abby was too booked up to give me an appointment, and I couldn't get a set time that coincided with my schedule. Perhaps Abby and I—an old married couple who'd ultimately been together for ten plus years— needed a break from one another. (Let she who has never wanted to put distance between herself and a person she loves throw the first roller.)

I was feeling spicy and decided that I wanted a new hair color. I'd never had a dramatic hair color change. Abby, as I've mentioned, put hair health above all else. Therefore, she'd always talked me down from the hair-coloring ledge. My hair was fine and dry and might be harmed by lifting it to a lighter color. But a girl wants what she wants. And surely a stylist I'd never used before would give me what I wanted, no questions asked.

The shop I found was on the second level of a small strip mall. Inside, the shop had the feminine touch of a proud black woman. African American art covered the walls. Gospel music blasted through a bulky speaker attached to the ceiling. I had an appointment with the owner, Carol, who was a studious-looking woman in her late forties with glasses and a short cut that mirrored my own. It was inspiring to me that so many black women owned their own shops, and it seemed to me that the older they were, the better the shop was run.

254

Carol gave me a magazine to pinpoint the hair color I wanted while I waited. It didn't take long for me to find the perfect hue. Talk-show host Star Jones stared back from the pages wearing an amazingly complex color that was a combination of honey blonde and gold highlights over a dark brown base. The color would make the stylish short cut I sported really pop.

I pointed to Star Jones's picture in the magazine. Carol merely glimpsed at the photo.

"Okay, that's fine," she said with cool professionalism. "Come to the bowl."

Carol escorted me a couple of steps to the shampoo bowl, then went to the back to mix the colors.

I was excited about getting this color. I'd imagined myself in it for years. Oprah's best friend, Gayle, rocked a similar multi-hued color, and I thought it would complement my skin tone well.

Carol returned. She worked efficiently, placing a piece of aluminum foil under sections of my hair, dabbing on the chemical concoction, then wrapping it in foil, section by section.

At this point, I'd been getting my hair done professionally for years. However, I was no expert. I didn't know the process for giving me the highlights I desired, but

I thought it was weird that all of my hair wasn't dyed a base color first—medium brown—and then sections highlighted. Oh, well. What did I know? Nothing. Perhaps after all of my hair was highlighted, she'd then throw a brown hue on top and that would give me the look I was hoping to achieve.

While the color saturated my hair, Carol left me so she could tend to her other clients.

"I'm leaving you in good hands," she said, and another, much older woman, came to ensure I was comfortable.

She and I engaged in small talk, and I learned that Elena was Carol's mother. Elena was a retired schoolteacher who busied herself during the day by helping her daughter run her shop. A black family-run business. How nice.

Elena peeked inside the foil. She closed it back up and went over to her daughter and whispered in her ear. Carol hurriedly set aside the blow-dryer and came over to check my hair.

Carol opened the foil and said, "Okay … It's done. You can wash her out and then condition her."

Oh, shit! Really? This bullshit again? I didn't want Elena servicing my hair. I wanted one person to tend my hair from start to finish.

Calm down, Rhonda. As long as you get the style you want who cares who washes your stupid hair?

Carol smiled at me and touched my shoulder. "Perfect. It looks really nice." Then she went back to her other client.

Let me see, letmesee, letmesee!

Elena began to wash and condition my hair. I had a fleeting wonder if she was licensed. I suspected not. If Elena was helping her daughter in the shop, I assumed Carol only had her mother doing as much as any shampoo girl would do and not anything that required mixing or applying harsh chemicals. An hour later, I had been washed and conditioned and was ready to sit in Carol's chair for drying and styling.

My entire body tingled as I headed toward the stylists' chair and the mirrors. I was about to debut my brand new hair color. The people at my job would be stunned by my glamour!

I looked in the mirror. Wait. Who the hell was that? Was that me? I stood in front of the mirror and stared at my wet hair in sheer disbelief. My hair was the color of a goddamned bumblebee.

"This isn't what I asked for," I said, unusually blunt. "What is this?"

Carol's eyes widened. "No, no. It's wet. It always looks a little different when it's wet. Sit, let me dry you."

I sat and fumed in silence until every fiber of my being radiated heat. I cannot say that I recall actual steam coming out of my ears, but I won't swear that it didn't. I stared at my reflection in the mirror. I knew damned well that no matter how dry my hair became it was never going to look like the picture. I watched her work at a rapid pace. Carol had screwed up. I knew it. And she knew it. She worked quickly with a quivering hand. Right now, there was nothing she wanted more than for me to be out of her chair, her shop, and her own damned hair.

And what about Abby? You mean to tell me I'd have to slink back to my regular stylist from whom I was taking an I'll-show-you-great-stylists-are-a-dime-a-dozen break and, with my tail between my legs and my Pittsburgh Steelers fangirl hair and beg her to fix it?

Not gonna happen. Carol had better know what she was talking about.

After what felt like an eternity, my hair was dry.

And don't you know, I still looked like a damn bumblebee.

Only now, I think it was worse because I could see even better that my hair didn't have a drop of honey blonde about it. My hair was a shimmery gold and black. No nuances of color, no depths, no highlights, no interesting blends, no complimentary hues. It was gold. And it was black.

"That's not what I asked for," I repeated, my leg bobbed up and down in irritation with such rapidity I probably looked like I suffered from some terrible disease.

The client in the chair next to me looked over at me with sympathetic eyes.

"Did you show her a picture of what you wanted?"

"Yes," I snapped, as Carol's fingers worked as quick as a marathon runner's legs with only a mile left in the race. "Here's the picture," I showed the woman next to me. "My hair looks absolutely nothing like this picture. Where's the brown? Where's the honey?"

"I'll tell you what we can do," Carol said nervously. "If you don't like the color you can come back in a couple of weeks, and I'll re-do it."

"Thanks, I'll be back," I said, miffed that I had to go to work and explain this exhibition on my head. Okay, fine. So I've had practice in that particular area. At least this time I *knew* it was a mistake.

I left the salon wondering if this was karma? Was this my fault for not sticking to the same hairstylist and settling my little conniving ass down? I knew Abby would have balked at putting highlights in my hair, and I had decided to go to someone who would. Was this my just desserts?

I was tempted to run to the corner pharmacy and buy a box of black hair dye to cover up my nicely styled but discolored hair.

Hey. Now there's a smart idea....

For the next two weeks, I strutted around Tampa with my super short, multi-striped haircut as though I was a trendsetter blazing a fashion trail instead of a woman muddling her way through a major hair faux pas. I did not buy black hair dye to cover up the mess for fear of seriously damaging my hair. Two weeks later, I stepped back into Carol's shop. She did a double-take and averted her eyes as soon as she saw me. She knew I was coming. I had an appointment. Had she thought I wouldn't return? Or was my ridiculous hair color burning her eyes? I kinda felt bad. We've all screwed up at work. I was a walking reminder of her mistake. Carol struck me as a genuinely kind professional who'd simply misunderstood what I wanted.

You will not be a bitch to her, Rhonda. Repeat. You will not be a bitch to her.

Carol and I talked politely about our lives as she applied a dark brown dye over my head. She was relaxed, friendly, and efficient. I noted her mother wasn't around that morning. When she was all done, my hair was better. Much better. But it wasn't remotely the golden-blonde-honey confection I had been aiming for. I tipped her for her services and left the shop pleased, both of us relieved we'd never have to see each other again.

The first thing Abby asked when I came back to her (tail between my legs, yada, yada, yada) was, "Who did your hair?"

"A lady named Carol. Do you know her?"

Abby shook her head and shrugged. This was the second major makeover I'd had done by a stylist other than Abby—first, the major chop, then this color.

"Why'd you color your hair?"

"I love that color Star Jones is rocking, and I wanted that color for myself."

"Color's not good for your hair," she said as though she'd never said it to me before.

"I know."

"And those black celebrities you see with all those beautiful colors, Beyoncé, Star Jones, Toni Braxton, they're not really coloring their hair all those colors, Rhonda."

"You don't think so?"

"I know so. They'd be bald. Those are wigs and weaves. At most they'll color a small portion of their hair to blend with a weave but they are not coloring their entire head those colors."

"Wigs?" I said, a new thought dawning on me. Wigs. That was a galaxy unexplored, land uncharted.

"Wigs," she said, seemingly unaffected by my infidelity. "Come to the washbowl. Let me fix this mess."

31

You will do foolish things, but do them with enthusiasm.

Sidonie Gabrielle Colette

Wiggy, wiggy, wiggy wiggy!

Wigs. It was a whole new world for me. I knew that entertainers wore wigs for their business. What I didn't know was that we were on the cusp of a wig revolution. Wigs were so good now that they were virtually undetectable. Lace-front wigs allowed women to rock long hair that could be parted anywhere on the wig and, if attached correctly, untrained eyes would be none the wiser.

Abby, a hair expert who kept her knowledge up by attending annual hair shows, already knew the score. I, on the other hand, was catching up to all the fun.

I decided to move into this new hair category slowly. By now, I was out of the military, working in the civilian world and occasionally dabbling in theater acting. I started with the half wigs. I'd plop a curly half wig attached to a cloth headband on my head, then pull it back slightly away from the front edges of my relaxed edges to give me a natural look. Talk about fun. But the styles for half wigs were few. Every day it would look as if you were wearing the same black band around your hair. How long could a girl stick with that look?

I made the big leap into the wig world by ordering what I thought was a cute, short, and sassy look from an online store. And it was the honey-blonde hue I'd been trying to achieve with my own hair. And now I could achieve that look in one-minute flat by plopping a wig on my head without risk of damaging my own hair. When the wig arrived I plopped it on my head and studied myself in the mirror.

Is this thing cute?

Does it make me look like a little old lady?

Does it look like a wig?

I wasn't sure. I couldn't be my own judge. These were still pre-Smartphone days so I couldn't snap a picture and send to my sister for her opinion. Instead, I emailed her the picture of the wig from the website.

"It looks cute on the model," she said.

Hmm. Yeah, but I most certainly was not the model. And didn't they have professionals cut the wigs to the models' heads? Should I have a professional cut the wig before I debuted it? Yeah, I probably should. It sounded like right ... so, naturally I went left. I had a better idea. Just take the damned thing out for a test drive. If no one's eyeballs made a beeline for my hair then it was probably okay.

I hopped in my Nissan Sentra and headed to the drive-thru of Dunkin' Donuts wearing my brand new wig. I placed my order for a double-toasted bagel with cream cheese and medium coffee. And then ... with my sister on the cellphone listening in ... I drove up to the window to pay.

The woman took my money and gave me my food. She barely glanced at me. That was a good thing, right?

"If she didn't look at you like you had a birds nest on your head then that's a good thing," Toya assured me. "I need to pop something on my head. But I don't feel comfortable wearing all that fake stuff."

"Why would you, of all people, want to do anything different to your hair?" I asked, remembering her baby-soft, long curly hair.

"All those years of relaxing has taken a toll on my head. Girl, I don't have the same hair I used to have back in the day. It's thin to the point of having a bald spot at the top of my head."

"Are you serious?"

"Bald spot," she said. "I may have to go to the dermatologist to find out what they can do. Did I tell you I'm using Rogaine?"

"Are you serious?" I replied, sipping my coffee and being a general nuisance on the road that Saturday morning. "I thought that was only for men."

"Nope, they have a female version. It's taking forever to work though." With no forewarning, the dam broke, and she began to cry. "What am I supposed to do without my hair?"

I remembered Toya as a teen beauty—a voluptuous Lolita who was never without the attention of the opposite sex. It's a tough pill to swallow—especially for a woman— to discover that looks are ephemeral. I had never been the male magnet that she was so when the time came for me to lose my hair, acquire wrinkles, or grow even more gray than I already was, I doubted I'd be quite as devastated as she was at the moment. As a person who'd suffered from facial acne, I never had any illusions about being any great beauty. Toya's good looks were very much a part of who she was as a person. It wasn't a wig she could plop on or plop off. It was always something she could rely on.

I offered her the only solution I could think of. "Toya, get a weave and keep it moving."

"I can't," she sobbed. "My hair is too thin. I can't braid this stringy mess."

"Or maybe get a wig. My wig looks really natural," I said, not wholly convinced that was true.

"I'm not like you, Rhonda," she said. She was finally getting a grip on herself as she explained her mindset. "I can't walk around and be okay with wearing fake hair."

I so enjoyed walking around with my occasional forays into fake hair that I couldn't work up the energy to feel offended. As far as I was concerned, my poor sister didn't know how much fun she was missing. Besides, she was losing her real hair. I couldn't imagine the devastation she was going through.

Toya continued, "I like wearing my own hair. And now it's going and...."

What followed was a high-pitched garbled mess as she melted down again. I pulled into my apartment complex and parked my car. I encouraged Toya to keep up with the Rogaine and to make a doctor's appointment. Honestly, until that conversation, I'd never known a dermatologist helped with hair issues. I'd seen a dermatologist as a teen and young adult for my acne, but to know they had real solutions that could help regrow hair was good information to keep in my back pocket. Considering my habitual hair antics, I'd need to make an appointment of my own soon enough.

I'd gone through a period where I was consumed with wigs to the point of going to a wig shop on my lunch hour, falling so in love with a wig that I wore it back to the office.

Oh, the looks.

Oh, the stares.

Oh, me and my foolishness.

Pure foolishness!

32

We keep moving forward, opening new doors, and doing
new things, because we're curious and curiosity keeps
leading us down new paths.

Walt Disney

New York, New York

One day I decided I didn't like my life. I remember sitting
in my cubicle at an accounting firm, searching the Internet
for something—anything—to occupy my time, when the
thought hit me: There has to be something more to life.
And it certainly wasn't in Tampa. At least not for me. I'd
had an idea brewing in the back of my mind all that year. In

that moment, I was inspired to make a go of it. I went online and started researching apartments in New York.

Holy Mother of Mizani. The rents were astronomical. I researched jobs—there were plenty of temporary opportunities if I couldn't find something permanent right off the bat. And I already had a car. I decided that if I was going to make the move, I'd need to do it fast, without giving it too much thought, or else I'd chicken out.

I had legitimate reasons for wanting to make the move to New York. I wanted to pursue my budding acting career. I'd gotten a good deal of work in Tampa and Orlando, and I wanted to try my chances in the big leagues. I also wanted to pursue a writing career. Books had been a childhood passion of mine, and I felt confident I could write one of my own. In New York, I'd be around other actors and writers I could learn from and be inspired by. I hadn't found the creative and cultural diversity in Tampa that I knew made New York the city that it was.

I was scared, of course. But I was also scared to go into the military, and I did it. I was scared to go to Saudi Arabia, but I did it. I was scared to get out of the military, but I did it. I stuffed my fear where I always do, deep in the bowels of my belly beneath the mountains of mint chocolate chip ice cream I'd consumed, and carried on. Maybe I was being a stupid little dreamer, but I knew I had to be that girl who tried. I was more scared of dying without trying to give my dreams a shot, than being that person who lived until her one-hundredth birthday without having tried shit. *That* scared me more than anything.

If the idea of relocating scared me, what was harder— downright difficult and completely against my personality—was asking for help. Nevertheless, I called my father.

"You're going to move to New York City? You know New Yorkers eat people like you for appetizers." My father chuckled at his own joke.

Standing over six feet, my father was a hulking man. As a little girl, I'd spend summers in Pittsburgh and then New Jersey with him and his wife. She was cool, but I was selfish. I wanted him all to myself. His sharp intellect, his quick wits were like sun shining on me. My father may have been a man of towering physical stature but so many things broke his heart: dishonest politicians, institutional racism, police brutality. He'd seen a lot of judicial injustice as a beat reporter in Pittsburgh. Before that, he'd seen horrific and unnecessary death in Vietnam. These were all sore subjects for him. Me? My future? It was a subject he delighted in because he thought the world was my oyster. All I needed to do was grab it.

"I think I'm tough enough," I said.

"I bet you are. You've been a karate-chopping combat cop in the A-R-M-Y." My father had been an airplane mechanic in the Air Force. To his great disappointment I'd followed in his shoes and joined the same military branch. He knew darned well I'd never spent a day in the A-R-M-Y. "Those New Yorka's had better move out of yo way. Rhonda Eason is coming to town!"

James, a serious intellectual, liked to cut loose at home and put on his terribly funny imitation of jive talk. I wondered if he ever let his guard down at the very corporate financial news magazine where he worked as an editor, and let his colleagues see that side of him? I'm sure he didn't. My father acted as though he carried the reputation of every black man on his shoulders. He would never let his guard down so much in corporate America.

"Whaddya need? You need some money?" he asked. He always asked if I needed money, and only once in my adult life had I taken him up on the offer. I felt weird doing so. He was my father and my idol, but he also lived in another state when I was a kid. There was an awkwardness to our relationship that we both had to learn to ignore. The one time he'd sent me money—I was about eighteen and living in England—I had sent him the $150 back via a check a couple of weeks later. My father was devastated.

"I can't believe you'd send me a check," he said. I'd never heard him so angry.

"I believe in paying my debts," I explained, taken aback by his response.

"You don't owe me anything, you understand?" he'd asked. "If you need something from me, you ask. You're my daughter. You don't ever have to pay me back."

I was speechless. He lived with the guilt of being an absentee father more than I knew.

Now, I said, "No. I don't need money. I'm dumping out my 401K and moving. I do need a place to stay though, until I get myself settled."

"Of course you can stay here," he said before I could even ask, without a moment of hesitation.

"Well, you don't have to tell me now. You can talk it over with Trina and see what she says."

My father chuckled at this. "I don't have to ask Trina anything. This is my house. You are my daughter. I'll clear out the extra bedroom for you. It has a small refrigerator in there and everything. When are you coming?"

My father's enthusiasm and total lack of anything resembling doubt or pessimism was infectious.

"As soon as I can get the money into my account, I'm out of here."

"Good girl. Well, I'd better start cleaning up your room."

Just as I didn't think of the things that awaited me in New York, I tried not to think too heavily on the things—the people—I would be leaving behind. I didn't formally dump my boyfriend; I simply said our long-distance romance was about to get really, really long. Both our relationship and friendship did what they sometimes do and fizzled out like a candle struck by a quick, cold wind.

And then there was Abby. Man how I hated leaving her. Believe me, if ever I was downright pissed that I wasn't rich enough to fly my hairstylist into my location at a moment's notice, it was then. But I wouldn't hinder my professional and personal goals because I wanted to stick close to my hairdresser. Hair had a big enough impact on my life. It wasn't going to stop me from achieving my goals.

"They have hairstylists on every corner," Abby said the last time she styled my hair. "I'm so excited for you. I hope you become famous. Did I tell you that I read your book?"

"*Secretary's Day*? You still have it?" I asked, incredulous.

"Yes, I liked it. It was good. I'm going to keep it so that when you're rich and famous I can say I knew you when."

Words she may never get to say, I thought.

Abby shot me her toothy grin through the mirror. I could tell she was genuinely happy for me. The moment reminded me of the scene at the end of *An Officer and a Gentleman* when Lynette cheered Paula on as Zack lifted Paula into his arms and carried her out of the factory and into their future. "Way to go, Paula. Way to go!" Lynette cried. Abby, a native New Yorker, was my Lynette. She talked fondly of the city all the time. She'd come to Tampa for new opportunities—what I was doing in reverse—and, although she was an independent shop owner, there was still an entire world of ethnic foods, diverse people, endless events that she'd left behind. And I was walking towards it. Between her and my father, I felt that I didn't even need to drive to New York. I could float there on a cloud of optimism.

In New York, I refused to reminisce about the dreadful experience I had in Tampa when I began looking for a permanent hairstylist. I would do as Abby suggested, walk my neighborhood until I stumbled upon a shop, avoiding the popular Dominican shops where I'd get my hair blow-dried super straight and bouncy but in about three months awaken to broken shreds of overheated wisps of hair.

I managed fairly well enough those first few months. I got into the weave game and found a shop that could give me a typical $150 weave install for the bargain basement price of sixty bucks. I went to my temp jobs looking decent with my cheap hair and cheaper install. Granted, I didn't look like Beyoncé, but I didn't look like Flyguy either. I didn't fall in love with a stylist, but I didn't encounter any who reduced me to tears either. I was actually doing it. I was a working girl in New York City!

And then I met a guy. A nice, sweet, handsome fella who, after only four months of dating, asked me that magical question that make us women swoon. "Rhonda, why don't you move in with me?"

Okay. Maybe *that* wasn't the particular question that makes us women swoon. And maybe his motivation had less to do with romance and more to do with fear for his life when he visited me in my sketchy neighborhood. Either way, my heart was already in the palm of his hand so I took the leap.

"Where can I get my hair done around this place?" I asked.

"You make Staten Island sound like it's in the middle of Antarctica," Marc said, driving toward his place. "You can get your hair done right there," he said pointing to a beauty salon that was a five-minute walk to his house.

Ha! I thought. No way would I ever be so lucky to find a *good* hairstylist that I *liked* only five minutes from my new love shack. God was good to me. But he'd never been *that* good.

Still. I called the shop, made an appointment with the owner, and soon after, I found my brand-new Abby and pretty much fell in love all over again.

33

A road to a friend's house is never long.
Danish proverb

Bye Felicia!

I sat inside the large beauty shop and tried hard to pretend I
didn't notice that Collette, the owner and beautician with
whom I had an appointment, hadn't made it to the shop yet.
I knew that as a stickler for timeliness, I needed to cut other
people some slack. Just because it was my habit to arrive
ten minutes early didn't mean everyone was the same.
Getting to the salon had proven to be one of the easiest

things I'd done since arriving in New York. Talk about a culture shock.

Whereas I was accustomed to hopping in my car, driving down Dale Mabry Avenue in medium to heavy traffic, and arriving at my employer's covered parking lot in about twenty-minutes time, now I lived in Staten Island and travelled to midtown for work, which meant a one-and-a-half hour to two-hour commute—*each way.* Things weren't much better when I lived in Brooklyn. I racked up towing charges and parking tickets because I couldn't adjust to the whole alternate-side-parking fiasco. Each day, drivers were required to move their cars by a certain time to the opposite side of the street so that street cleaners could come by and tidy up. The irony is that the streets never looked particularly clean to me, but whatevs. I found the ordeal of having to drive blocks away from my apartment to find a parking space antiquated and unnecessary, and as a young woman who couldn't parallel park to save her life, it made the already impossible task a cruel punishment for even having a car. And the parking signs ... so many parking signs! I came to New York armed with a bachelor's degree, but it seemed I needed a master's to understand the plethora of parking signs with all those damned rules. Did I really have to read and *obey* the signs? I was in New York now, which meant that I was big-time New Yorka (written in my father's playful big-shot tone) so why would I have to follow the rules? If it suited me, I parked in front of bus stops and private driveways. And I got towed or ticketed every time. Those meter maids were on their game. I couldn't outsmart them. I was never sure what New York State of Mind meant, but if it referred to a general sense of feeling bewildered and beleaguered, then yeah, I was there.

So the five-minute walk to the beauty salon was a gift from God, especially since I'd sold my car. (It was clear to me that the New York establishment was against mere mortals like me having cars anyway—what with their rules and limited parking.) My beautician's hands might also have been a gift from God, but how could I possibly know until she deigned to come to work and get busy on my head? While I waited I watched the other stylist tend to a client. There was something about her—a woman about ten years my senior—that drew me to her. Maybe it was the ever-ready gapped-tooth smile that reminded me of Abby's own quick, toothy grin. Maybe it was the care she was giving her client's hair, never really satisfied that it fell just-so even though it looked pretty damned good to me. Maybe it was the way her oversized glasses rested on her plump cheeks, covering her beady eyes, but not quite obscuring the fact that nothing escaped them. She saw me sitting there, waiting for Collette to arrive. Her occasional smile in my direction acknowledged my existence while at the same time seemed to say, *I just rent a booth from her, so I'm gonna stand here and mind my own business.*

Finally, Collette arrived through the front door with an infectious smile of her own and a soft, throaty voice.

"I'm sorry," she said when she entered. "You want to go ahead and have a seat in my chair?"

"Sure," I said.

Collette had a sweet energy about her, and it was hard for me to be upset. We chatted while she applied my relaxer. I learned that she was very active in the church, married with two kids, and apparently a fine singer, oftentimes leading her church choir at events around the state and beyond. Collette was a hustler. Many New Yorkers were, I'd noticed. They balanced their day jobs with their passion jobs. One paid the bills, the other fed the soul.

Over the next few weeks, I was neither overly impressed nor disappointed in her work. She was good. I didn't require much—a relaxer, a black rinse to cover my gray, and a trim. She did the job suitably enough, and I was pleased. She was detached from me, acting more as a robot than a beautician who wanted a friendship, but that was fine by me. If she came in late a few times or ran behind schedule, so be it. That was nothing compared to the horrors that I'd endured in Tampa.

Nevertheless, when I sat in her chair, I couldn't help staring at the other beautician's work. I didn't know her name. I simply watched the customers as they left her chair and was always a tad disappointed that I wasn't sitting there. If Collette was smoke, then the other beautician was fire. I was suffering from serious hairdresser envy.

One day when I came into the salon, I had an issue with my hair that I wanted to discuss with Collette, but I decided to wait until she brought up the subject. Perhaps I was doing this as a kind of test. Abby, who constantly consulted me about my hair health, had set the bar high for all the stylists who would come after her. I expected someone to tell me about the general condition of my hair or, at the very least, any issues that she noticed and make recommendations.

I sat flabbergasted in Collette's chair when she made the finishing touches to my hair by spraying me down with oil sheen. Was she really not going to say anything?

"Um, did you notice that I'm losing my hair in the back?" I asked.

"What? Where?"

Not the right answer. Not even close. How the heck can you put a relaxer in my hair, trim my hair, style my hair and not notice the one-inch bald swatch at the nape of my neck?

"Right here," I said, lifting my hair.

"Oh, wow," she said as though I were showing her a profane tattoo in my secret garden.

"It's from my winter coat," I said. "This has happened before, and I forget that I need to wear silk scarves," I said casually although I started to fume inside. "What do you think I should do in the meantime? Should I cut my hair?"

I had been growing my hair out of my cute little Nia Long haircut. It's a similar cut to the one Collette was currently rocking (very well, I might add.)

"You could. I'm very good at cutting hair, and you'd look good with a short cut. You have the right face for it."

"Hmm," I thought. She hadn't provided me a lick of insight. Did she really not notice my missing hair? It's so obvious because my hair doesn't even hang correctly in the back because so much is missing at the nape of my neck.

I departed the shop graciously, but I was annoyed. For days I kept thinking, how was it possible for a stylist not to notice a bald spot?

One of Collette's habits (that I was trying hard to overlook) was that she conversed and gossiped with her clients while I was in the chair. Perhaps this is my own selfishness in play, but I believed the client in your chair should be the person to get your attention, and perhaps your conversation, not the person who dropped in and sat in the empty chair next to the client, keeping the stylist entertained. I didn't make a big deal about Collette chatting with other people while she styled my hair. I regarded it as rude, but as long as she was keeping my hair healthy and nice-looking, I didn't care. I'd been through worse. But the fact that she didn't notice my bald spot was on a whole other level.

That incident was at the forefront of my mind when I visited her again. I got to the shop on time and was told by the other stylist that she hadn't made it in yet. It was the first time I noticed she had a thick accent. Was she West Indian? New York had a large population of West Indians. I plopped down on the ripped black pleather sofa and waited for Collette. And I waited.

"Do you have her number?" the stylist asked, concern in her eyes.

"Yeah," I said, "I left her a voicemail that I was here waiting for her."

"I don't know where she could be," the woman said.

And you know what? I didn't care where she could be. The small things that I'd been overlooking had started to build up. Collette routinely avoided conversation with me. She was habitually late. And, worse and most unforgivable of all, she didn't notice my bald spot.

"Do you have any appointments available?" I asked the beautician.

Her eyes widened before she averted them. Her short wig seemed to display the shock she was feeling as its wild curls stuck up in every direction. Yep, I was probably about to start some ish, and I didn't care one wit.

"Uh, well, um … not today."

"That's fine," I said, not about to be deterred. "What about next Saturday?"

"Uh, well, um … yeah, let me get my book." She set down the hot curlers that were in her hand with the speed of a turtle in a long-distance marathon. She was racked with indecision, and I didn't care. I was a customer who needed a stylist. She was a stylist. What was the problem? "Are you sure you don't want to wait on Collette?"

"I'm sure," I said with a tight smile on my face.

"Next Saturday at … eight?" she asked me. I bet she was hoping I was going to say that was too early.

"Perfect! I'll see you then. By the way, what's your name?"

"Lily. And you are?"

"Rhonda. Nice to meet you, Lily. I've been watching your work, and I can't wait to sit in your chair. See you next week!"

"Let me see if I got this straight," Toya said to me on the phone between incredulous laughter. "You plan to go into the same shop and sit in another beautician's chair? With your old beautician standing right there?"

"Yep, sure do."

"Rhonda, you're terrible."

"How? It's my hair. I own it, and I can have anybody style it."

"Yeah, but...." she sighed. "Rhonda, go to a different shop."

"Why should I put myself through that when there's a perfectly capable person in walking distance of my house?"

"So you're just gonna walk right past Collette and go sit in Lily's chair?"

"Uh huh, yep, sure am.

"I have to say, I get sick of my lady sometimes, and I want to sit in somebody else's chair. But I don't have the

286

balls to do that to her. My lady makes my curls so tight I leave looking like I'm wearing one of Grandma's old wigs. I have to go home and restyle my hair."

"Tell her you want looser curls."

"I did. She wants to give me curls that lasts all day."

"Girl, you're paying *her*. You should get what you want."

"Well, you let me know what happens next week."

"What do you think Collette's going to do? Run me out of the shop?"

"Yep."

The next weekend, I bound toward the shop, ready for Lily to do my hair. The closer I got the more I thought about my conversation with Toya. Was I the crazy one in this scenario? Collette was habitually late, didn't see or didn't care about my bald spot, and I'm supposed to keep paying her for the privilege? Nope.

I arrived at the shop. Collette wasn't there yet. *Naturally.* I sat in Lily's chair, and we got along famously. She told me she was from Africa, no kids, married. I felt a kinship to her since I wasn't far behind her in age, also lived child-free, and enjoyed a pretty solid relationship. Even though she had no children of her own, Lily was a maternal type of a person, warm, who seemed to be created expressly to hold family secrets, give good advice, provide a listening ear and a soft hug.

Collette entered the shop. She did a double take when she saw me laughing my head off in Lily's chair. I wasn't trying to act like a mean girl. I was sincerely enjoying Lily's company. Not to mention that Lily was talking to *me,* not to other people milling around her chair. She gave each of her client's personal attention.

Collette and I smiled civilly at each other, spoke, and carried on as if it was just another Saturday at the shop.

"Was it just because she was late?" Lily finally asked me.

"No. That bald spot you mentioned earlier went completely unnoticed by her. I mentioned it to her when she was done with my hair, and she acted as if she hadn't seen it."

"That does not surprise me," Lily said. "She is good—very good—at cutting hair short and maintaining those styles. Notice her clients. They all have short cuts. They didn't start out that way. She talks them into it. She was probably going to wait for the right time to suggest she cut off all your hair."

"Are you serious?"

"Hmm," Lily said. "You're not the first client of hers to come to me," she said. "It gets hard because she thinks I'm stealing her clients. I don't steal clients. They come to me. Always. I don't like drama."

"Do you think it would be best to cut my hair a little though?"

"We don't need to cut your hair, sweetie. We'll get it back the way it was before and make it better. Trust me. You're in good hands."

"Thanks, Lily."

I've been thanking her for a dozen years.

34

Less is more.

Ludwig Mies van der Rohe

A Wig Too Far

I remember the day I fell in love. With a wig. I'd gone into a hair supply store and fell fantastically in love with a wig that called to mind Diana Ross's hair at her iconic performance in Central Park.

"Why don't you try it on?" the young girl said to me.

That's a comment you don't usually hear in a hair supply store that specializes in black hair care. Oftentimes owned by Asian-Americans, these stores are notorious for having employees follow customers around the aisles from the moment they step inside the store to the second they step out. And I've never experienced any of them suggesting I try on a wig. The feeling was generally: make your selection quick, pay, get out. In fact, many stores have a three-wig try on limit. Huh? Whatever. I had more freedom walking through a prison than I did a black hair supply store. You'd think grease and five-dollar packs of braid hair were the Holy Grail. This was why most of my wig purchases were made online. Who needed to be reminded that in someone's eyes I was less of a customer and more of a potential criminal?

And this young Hispanic girl was also following me. But she had a friendly customer-service oriented demeanor. Maybe if she hadn't smiled so encouragingly I would have only noted the beauty of the wig and kept moving. No, I know this wasn't true. Not the way my heart was pounding at the sight of it.

"Okay, yeah, sure."

I put the wig on, turned in the mirror. It was black, big, and hit me in the middle of my back. The curls were springy and voluminous, much like the hair of the girl assisting me. It felt like cotton candy to my soul.

"That looks nice on you!" she said emphatically.

I thought so too. I mugged in the mirror and smiled.

"How much is it?"

"Only sixty dollars."

I hadn't come to the beauty salon to get a sixty-dollar wig. I'd come for shampoo. Sixty dollars on fake hair wasn't in the budget.

"Really cute. You look like Lisa Bonet in *Angel Heart.*"

If you do not know what Lisa Bonet looks like, please take this moment to Google her in the aforementioned film. Done? Okay. Now that you know what *she* looked like, let me give you an idea of what I looked like. Staring back at me in the mirror was a brown complexioned woman, topping out at five-two, with middle-aged plump around the tummy, a petite round-tipped nose and a smattering of chin hair that begged to be cut. The only part of me that even remotely looked like Lisa Bonet was my pupils.

The young girl continued, "The resemblance is uncanny."

And I said, with the same giddiness of a brand new million-dollar lottery winner, "I'll take it."

I didn't need much of an excuse for going into the city. I had my new hair on, and it was the boldest look I'd ever had. I needed to get out and test drive that baby like it was a brand new Ducati. The next day, a Sunday, I hopped on the Staten Island ferry bound for lower Manhattan. I was bummed out by the fact that Marc didn't get a chance to see me before I left. All the better for me to surprise him when I got home.

I know that feeling that Julia Robert's had in *Pretty Woman* when the theme song of the same name played as she walked. She felt like the most beautiful and luckiest girl on the planet. I, too, was a pretty woman, walking down the streets of New York, as men turned to check me out.

I know, right? I thought as I returned a pleasing head nod.

My hair bounced in the breeze behind me as I made my way from block to block, looking for nothing, just enjoying the summer warmth and wanting to be seen. And I was. It was the hair. I couldn't wait to debut this gorgeous mane at work the next day. People were going to be stunned at my fierceness.

I got even more excited as I got closer to home. I wasn't going to say a word to Marc. I'd just waltz into the house as if nothing was amiss and pretend I didn't notice his eyes ogling me, *wanting* me.

"Hey, what's up?" I asked, flicking on the light and interrupting the mood he'd set as he watched television.

"Hey," he said after a beat. He pulled his eyes away from the flat screen and gazed silently at me. Intensely. It's the kind of gaze we women dream of. I mean, I thought it was the kind of gaze we dream of. It looked a tad ... off.

Keeping to my plan, I sashayed through the house removing my clothes, pulling on PJs, knocking around in the kitchen. Our house was small. Marc could have spoken to me from any part of the place and I could've heard him. He was quiet. Eerily so. Was that pent-up passion?

I went back into the living room and glanced at him as I busied myself with feeding the dog. He still gazed at me, but this time he had a pained look on his face, as though a fowl Pepe Le Pew odor emanated from my backside.

Done with my chores and with a bowl of cereal in my hand, I joined him on the sofa. Slowly, he turned his head to look at me.

"What is that?"

"What is what?" I asked.

"That!" Marc pointed to my head as though it were a dead rat I'd decided to plop up there instead of my Diana Ross inspired wig.

"It's my new hair," I said, still bubbling over with joy. "Don't you like it?"

"No," he said as if there was no possibility of that ever happening. "Wait," he said, a light dawning in his eyes. "You wore that outside?"

"Yes," I said defensively. "I just came back from the city. And for your information, men were staring at me left and right."

"Yeah," Marc said, "because you look like a crackhead. They were probably wondering how much you charge."

My jaw dropped. Did I mention that Marc only *looks* like a sweetheart but inside he's a cruel, cold soul? You'd have to be to say something so sacrilegious about that amazing hair.

"Well...." I said, trying to take his crappy critique seriously. What did he know about hair? "I was thinking about cutting it. Make it a little shorter."

"Uh huh," he said, shaking his head. "Take it off and burn it."

"Marc! I paid sixty dollars for this hair."

"You got ripped off."

"The girl at the store told me I looked great."

"Is it her job to sell wigs?"

"Well...."

"Bamboozled," he said.

"She said I looked like Lisa Bonet."

"Get the hell outta here. Have you seen yourself lately?"

"You know what? You suck. and I don't like you anymore."

"Look. You do what you need to do, but I'm telling you, you look terrible with that hair on your head. What's wrong with your own hair?"

"I get bored with my own hair."

"Well that thing is not the right solution. It looks terrible. Now you can never say you didn't know."

I got up from the sofa and went into the bathroom to inspect myself.

Okay, maybe Lisa Bonet was a stretch.

I turned my head to the side. But when I turned it back to look at myself in the mirror, I didn't see myself at all.

Instead, oh, my Lord.

I saw Flyguy.

35

Camouflage is a game we all like play, but our secrets are
as surely revealed by what we want to seem to be as by
what we want to conceal.

Russell Lynes

Where Are You?

When it came to hair, Lily and I were two kids in a candy
store. She loved hair, loved her work, loved the satisfaction
of transforming her clients. I had a certain kind of rebirth
under Lily's care. Whereas my desire to change came
sporadically with Abby, now I could hardly be tamed. We
were children experimenting with all kinds of hairstyles,

mainly of the weave variety. There were short weaves and long weaves and curly and straight and cheap and outrageously expensive (for my budget.) There was almost no hairstyle she couldn't get me to consider (except one of her fancy ponytails because, as I've mentioned I hate static hair.)

With each new hairstyle came a new iteration of me. Perhaps I was motivated to change because of the sheer originality I saw displayed amongst my fellow sistas in New York. There was no limit of imagination on display. Although I worked in a corporate environment and kept my styles in line with my profession, I pushed the envelope when it came to a number of styles. Every other month one could expect to see a new me walk through the doors. I knew it was awkward for my coworkers—particularly the Caucasians—to wrap their brain around this constant transformation. Luckily, I worked with other black women, and a few of them kept pace with the rapidity of my quick change. In New York, I had found my people.

Marc did his best to keep pace with the change, too. He didn't understand it. Didn't particularly like it. But I was sweet and funny and sexy and ambitious, and he couldn't let a woman like *that* slip out of his grasp, now could he?

We were together one Sunday afternoon, running errands and generally enjoying the summer weather. We stopped at the market to pick up a few groceries.

"You know, this would go a lot faster if you picked up some items, and I picked up others, and we met back up at a central location," he said.

The grocery store to Marc was like a baseball game to me. It didn't make any sense, and right when you thought it was over, it dragged on into eternity.

"Fine," I said and sent him off with a short list of items that he could memorize and bring back to the cart easily in his hands. After I was done with my part of the shopping, I checked my watch. Surely, he'd been gone for ten minutes by now. The grocery store wasn't even that crowded for a Sunday afternoon. I dug out my phone, but I didn't have any missed calls. I wouldn't bother him either. Chances are his phone was on silent anyway. Marc's phone was *always* on silent. I think it was his way of saying "Don't call me, I'll call you."

I had an idea. I'd position myself at the front of the store and walk by each of the aisles until I spotted him. He had to be down one of them. Slowly, I walked past each of the aisles, looking for him. When I got to the end of the store I started to grow concerned. Did he go to the checkout instead? I decided to give the walking past the aisle idea another shot. Finally, I looked down the empty expanse of an aisle and saw Marc apparently doing the same thing I was doing, but at the opposite end of the store. Then, to my complete surprise, Marc sucked his teeth, shook his head and walked toward the next aisle.

What the—?

Marc had looked directly at me and kept going. What was *that* about?

Finally, he made his way up to the front of the store. My sense of humor had left me awhile ago.

"What was that?"

"What was what?" he asked. "I've been looking all over for you."

"I was right there," I said, pointing to the spot that I'd stood like Casper the Friendly Ghost only moments before. "You looked directly at me and kept going."

"Look," he said, shaking his head. "I looked down the aisle for a short, black girl with straight hair. I looked down the aisle, I didn't see that person, I kept walking."

"What are you saying?" I asked. "We've been together for three years, and you don't know what I look like?"

"You change your hair so much that I can't always remember!"

"Are you saying you couldn't pick me out of a lineup?"

"I'm saying I might send the wrong person to jail because you keep changing up your hair. Why do you do that anyway?"

I couldn't believe we were having this conversation in a checkout line of a grocery store.

"I like change," I said.

"I don't get it. I really don't. White women get a nice hairstyle that they like in college, and they keep it for the rest of their lives. My mother? She did the same thing. I don't understand why every two months I'm looking at a completely different person with a bunch of wacky hairdos."

Marc didn't get my need for change. It was understandable. I didn't completely get it either. It was as though I was chasing a butterfly that kept eluding me.

"You don't like my hair?"

Marc looked at my new weave and weighed the consequences of his next words. Obviously feeling brave, he said, "No."

"No?" I said. "When I asked you if you liked my hair, you said yes."

"I lied. I don't like it. You had a nice hairstyle before. Why'd you change it?"

"You lied?"

"You were happy with the lie," he reminded me. "I told you what you wanted to hear."

I was taken off guard, but not altogether offended. I was more upset about the fact that he couldn't recognize a woman that he lived with than that he didn't like my hair. I don't get my hairstyles for him to like. I get hairstyles for me to like, and if he does too, bonus.

But the whole episode got me to thinking. Why *did* I have to change up so often? I wasn't an actress going from one movie role to another. I wasn't a singer whose ever-changing image was directly related to her relevance. Now that I really thought about it, even celebrities tend to make small changes to their style without doing a complete one-eighty. They would keep the same cut for a year but add waves, add a bang, remove a bang, add a subtle highlight here, a lowlight there. My changes were as drastic as taking off a Dior evening gown and putting on a bikini from Walmart and then changing out of that into an Ann Taylor pants suit. It didn't make any sense! And yet, in some weird way, it made perfect sense. I was still the kid with a shirt on her head except now all my fantasies could come true. I was changing styles as though I wouldn't be able to get through them all before I died.

And the styles—oh Lord—the *styles*! I've had a head full of gold-colored kinky twists that I'd gotten done at a braid shop in Harlem. Two braiders knocked out an eight-hour braid style in half the time and left me looking like I belonged to a 1980s girl band. A terrible one at that. It was a ridiculous amount of braids on top of my head. A few times I'd found one of the twists had slipped out of my head. There it would be, on the floor, looking like a dead snake on the carpet. Fine, if this happened at the house. But a couple of times, I'd be walking around my office, look down and—Oh, Jesus! I'd swoop up the fallen braid and ball it into a fist, wondering if anyone had seen it and thought, "Hmm. That looks like part of Rhonda's new hairdo on the floor. I'll leave it there for her to retrieve."

Marc was sick of the variety. Okay, I got it. Why hadn't he told me that before? Would I have changed my modus operandi if he had? Was I in any way obligated to consider his opinion of my changing looks? The feminist in me said hell no. I could look how I wanted, when I wanted, for whatever reason I wanted.

But what if I looked ridiculous? There are people who can walk the earth with black lipstick and purple hair and tattoos on their face because they don't care about other people's opinion. They *want* to stand out. Fashion visionaries make their living by being different and adventurous. However, I'm conservative by nature. It isn't in me to wear something outlandish so that all eyes in the room turn to me. I don't want all eyes on me. So what's with the multitude of hairstyles? Was I still trying to find my perfect self? How foolish was I willing to look in order to find it? Would I ever find *the hairstyle* that would allow me to settle into my skin and stop searching for something better?

Or would I die trying?

36

We often give our enemies the means to our own
destruction.

Aesop, "The Eagle and the Arrow"

Therapy

At some point in 2013, I found myself sitting in a
therapist's office. Hey, don't judge. If you worked in an
intellectually unstimulating job with a bunch of gossipy,
mean-spirited secretaries you'd find yourself on a
therapist's couch, too. Jenny wore her thick, curly brown
hair in a ponytail. She sipped hot tea and kept a shawl
draped loosely around her shoulders, as her soft gray eyes
studied me with warm regard.

"Something's different about you," she said, not quite able to put her finger on the change.

I'd been going to her every other week for about three months and felt that she was a bit too nice to be an effective therapist. I needed a therapist who told me straight up what my problem was, asked me the tough questions that cut to the heart of the matter. That wasn't Jenny's style. She was more like a nurturing sounding board. Still, it was good to talk to someone who was paid to sit and listen.

"My hair," I said, anxious to get to the work-related issues I'd come to whine about. "It's different."

That day I was rocking a Farrah Fawcett inspired weave that I thought made me look like a vixen.

Jenny sipped her tea, then considered my hair. "Yeah, it was different before. Did you cut it?"

At this point in my life, this question was a phenomenon I'd experienced with white people on numerous occasions. I could go from one-inch to sixteen-inches of hair over the span of a weekend, and when they saw me for the first time since the transformation the question would always be: "Did you cut your hair?" Apparently, I gave off Rapunzel vibes no matter what hairstyle I rocked.

"No," I said patiently. "It's a weave. Before I just had my hair relaxed."

She frowned. "Hmm. I thought you had braids."

Oh, come on Jenny! Keep up, will you? That was six sessions ago. "Um, no. I had the braids the first time I came to see you. Then I had a relaxer. Now I have a weave."

"Hmm," she said again. She paused a beat, then asked, "Do you always change your hair so often?"

"Yeah, I do," I said. I felt my heart start to beat double time, a sure sign of my defensiveness. Even I knew that without a therapist's input. I hadn't come to talk about my hair because my hair had nothing to do with my psychology, my current emotional state, or the problems I was having with the bitchy bullies at my job who were making me feel terrible about myself. "My hair is just fun, like make up. It doesn't mean anything," I explained. "I get bored with my looks so I like to change it up sometimes." Inexplicably, I was beginning to sweat, even though her office was frigid. And I rambled non-stop. "My hair is an expression of myself. I've loved hair since I was a kid. I love to play in hair, so that's why I'm constantly switching things up."

Jenny looked at me as if my toes hovered over the highest point of the Brooklyn Bridge. "Okay, okay." She shrugged, as if to say: *If that's what you think, fine. I'll let you keep telling yourself that story.* "What brings you here today?"

"I'm not myself ever since I started working this job. I'm losing who I am, and it's really starting to bother me."

"How so?"

"The women at my job—the other secretaries—are vicious. They gossip constantly, and a lot of times it's about me, and I've ignored it as much as I can."

"The gossip is oftentimes about you? How do you know?"

"Well, I don't know for a fact. But I sit next to a girl, and I can hear her on the phone talking about me."

"She says your name?"

"No," I said, frustrated. Why was she being so dense? "You can just tell when someone's talking about you. For example, if I send an email with the slightest mistake in it, say I write Thursday, March 22nd, and Thursday is actually the 23rd, she'll pick up the phone and start laughing about it with the other secretary down the hall. It's so incredibly immature. These women are over thirty-five years old; one is nearing fifty!"

"So they're petty, immature. Why let it bother you so?"

"I'm human. It's kind of hard to not let something like that bother you. It's almost as if it's bullying. They're emotional terrorists."

Emotional terrorists. That was a new phrase I'd learned from my sister who was describing our mother. I adopted it as my own.

"Have you read that book I told you about a while ago?"

"No," I admitted. She'd recommended I read *The Four Agreements* by Don Miguel Ruiz. I hadn't gotten around to reading it.

"You're a very bright girl, Rhonda. I recommend you read it. I think a lot of the issues you raise are addressed in that book. You're someone who could really appreciate it."

I assured her I'd read it. (By the way, I did read it, and she was right. I no longer needed her services after doing so. At least, not for feeling bullied at work.)

"So," she continued, "you feel as if these women are affecting your self-esteem. Making you doubt your skill level and making you feel bad about yourself?"

"They make me feel unsure about myself, yes. And I have a very high self-esteem."

This intrigued her. She glimpsed at my hair and then asked, "You have a high self-esteem?"

"Yes," I said. "Of course I do. I've always had a very high self-esteem. I act, remember? I get on stage in front of hundreds of people, and it doesn't intimidate me at all."

"Yes, but when you're acting, aren't you someone else? You present someone else when you're on stage or in front of the camera. You read someone else's words. So when people judge, they're really not judging Rhonda."

"They're judging my acting."

"Yes, but isn't your acting separate from who you are as a being?"

"Yeah, I guess."

"To act takes courage, certainly, but so does bungee jumping. But couldn't someone with a low self-esteem be a bungee jumper?"

"I guess," I said, slightly annoyed with the fact that she was questioning my high self-esteem. That was one of the things I'd always known for sure about myself. Now I wasn't so certain.

"Do you think it's possible that the women at your job might be a little jealous of you?"

"Pssh, no," I said with a snort. "Why would they be jealous of me? I'm a secretary just like they are."

"You act. You audition and someone chooses you for roles, right?"

"My acting is small time."

"You're a writer."

"That's small time too," I refuted.

"You're a published author."

In the six years since I'd arrived in New York, I'd continued building my writing skills. I'd managed to self-publish two books, and a publisher picked up one of them.

"My publisher is small," I said dismissively.

"Rhonda. A professional editor read your work and thought it was worthy of publishing. You don't think that's significant?"

"It's cool," I said. "I'm really happy about it, and I think it's very validating. But no one reads what I write."

"Okay, so aside from your achievements: serving in the military, graduating college, becoming a published author, acting, being pretty, being independent, you don't think you have anything worthy of envy? You believe those women are picking on you because of typos?"

"Well, I mean, when you put it like that...."

Jenny adjusted her hands around her steaming mug. "How many secretaries did you work with at the job before this one?"

"This is the first time I've worked with a large number of secretaries. At this job I work with about ten secretaries

311

on my floor alone. At my last job, it was only two of us. Before that, only about four."

"Hmm … so you're in a larger pool of women and have more personalities to deal with, and it's a bit overwhelming."

"I'm shocked that women can be so old and so incredibly catty. I get to work, sit in my hole and work and think about my future, what I want for myself. Listen," I said, circling back around to her comments about my high—high?—self-esteem. "I'm not the kind of person who has a low self-esteem. I'm constantly working hard to improve myself. That isn't what a person with a low self-esteem looks like."

"What does a person with a low self-esteem look like?"

I hesitated, trying to conjure up my idea of a person who thought little of herself.

"A stripper. Strippers have low self-esteem."

"All strippers?"

"Yeah, pretty much. Or why else would they dance naked on a pole for men to gawk at?"

"Is it possible that there are some strippers who think they are beautiful enough to be admired and choose to dance as a way of making income?"

"All that, plus their daddies weren't around, hence a low self-esteem."

"I thought you said your father wasn't around."

Ouch.

"He was. He was a very positive influence in my life, but I mostly saw him in the summers when he'd send a plane ticket so I could visit."

"Right, that's right," she said as though a bulb had clicked in her head. "That must have been difficult visiting your kind of well-to-do father in the summers, then going back home to be with your financially struggling, single mother for the rest of the year. Completely different lifestyles. Do you think that had any bearing on you, not being rooted in a secure family atmosphere?"

"Maybe" I said. I hadn't really thought about it.

"Did you have to act one way around your mother and another way around your father?"

"I don't think so."

"You don't think so?"

"No."

"Okay," she said.

Sounds from the ambient noise machine she kept in the hallway seemed to have gotten louder all of a sudden.

313

"I think we can end here. Let's meet again in two weeks," she said, consulting her appointment book. "I can't wait to see how pretty your hair will be then."

37

Revolution is as unpredictable as an earthquake and as
beautiful as spring. Its coming is always a surprise, but its
nature should not be.

Rebecca Solnit

A New Revolution

I remember the exact day that I tuned into a cultural
revolution that was happening around me. I was sitting in
the quaint waiting room of my holistic practitioner's office
over in New Jersey. The company was run by a married
African American couple. Both were devout believers in
the holistic lifestyle that included a vegan diet and regular
detoxifications. They both wore their hair in dreadlocks.

The last time I'd seen Derek his dreads were brushing his shoulders. Now, only a few short months later, they reached the middle of his back. That in itself was a testament to his healthy lifestyle. I had been seeing him for a few months, slowly dipping my toes into the world of colonics, and, once over the gross factor, actually enjoyed the ritual.

On that particular day, I was there to pick up my supplies for the ten-day fast I was about to start. I sat in the waiting room with two other women about my same age. Their feet soaking in a detoxifying footbath while they chatted.

"Girl, I can't believe people are still putting those chemicals on their head," said one woman. I glanced at her and noticed her hair was in a short, shameful-looking afro. It looked like it hadn't been picked or oiled in a month.

"Ignorance," said the other woman. Her hair was also styled in dreads. Unlike Derek and Kat's, her hair looked matted and unkempt. She continued, "Black women trying so hard to look like they people came from Brazil instead of Africa. Ain't foolin' nobody."

My people came from Augusta and Pittsburgh. Cotton and steel mills. And I wasn't trying to fool anybody. My hair, by the way, was freshly relaxed at the top and blended into my spanking new weave that Lily installed the day before. My hair was on point. If I had to spend a day with my hair looking unkempt like either of those women, I'd jump off a moving subway train. But I got their point.

As I sat there listening to the two of them bash me and women like me, I wondered if their sense of superiority permeated throughout the black community? Had I missed something?

When I got home I researched natural hairstyles and blogs. I was surprised to learn that, indeed, there was a cultural revolution occurring right under my nose. More black women were ditching relaxers in favor of maintaining their own hair. These women, by in large, were not ditching wigs, weaves or braids as these were considered "protective" styles. Protective styles allow a woman to keep heat and chemicals off her real hair while wearing these alternative hairstyles, thereby protecting the natural hair.

And yes, by scrolling through the comments section, I could see that there were some all-natural women who deemed themselves superior to those of us who opted to keep relaxing our hair.

"What are you doing?" Toya asked me. She'd called me up to gossip about work.

"I'm looking through a bunch of pictures of natural hairstyles, and I love them."

"It's a handful. I've been natural for fifteen years, and I'm telling you I'd do anything to get my relaxer back."

"Why don't you?"

"Rhonda. I was going bald! I have to preserve what little hair I have left. I've been getting shots in my scalp on and off at the dermatologists office for fifteen years now, trying to save my hair."

"I can't imagine a needle going into your scalp."

"If it sounds like it hurts, that's because it does. I get a series of six shots. But, it does make my hair grow back."

"I loved your natural hair. If I had your hair I never would've gotten a relaxer."

"I'm not a fan of natural hair. Never have been, never will be. Guess what I bought yesterday?"

"Ben and Jerry's?"

"No, but I should pick some up today," she said, too easily distracted by the thought of food.

"What'd you buy?"

"A wig!"

"No way. You hate wigs and weaves."

"Not anymore. I went into the beauty supply store with my niece Nikki, and she got me to try on a wig, and it looks *exactly* like mine when I have a relaxer. So I got it."

"You're going to go into the office with it on tomorrow?"

"Yep. You think people will notice?"

"Um...." Should I be honest or make her feel better? I decided on honesty. "Yeah, probably. But the point of a wig isn't necessarily to look like you're not wearing one. Everybody knows Rihanna doesn't have red hair down to her behind. The point is to look and feel good wearing it."

"Yeah, I guess. Anyway, I love it! It really does look like my own hair."

"Good luck," I said, distracted by the beautiful images of natural hairstyles on my computer.

A year later, I still had my relaxers and weaves. Who was I kidding? I wasn't a natural type of girl. However, I had started taking a second look at the black women in New York. More and more of them were wearing their hair natural. Some styles were fantastic, some were 'eh', and some were downright unkempt and frightening. I couldn't chance that even if I wanted to. (And I kinda wanted to.)

By then, I'd all but forgotten about those women in the holistic center and gotten on with my life.

My niece, Nikki, and a girlfriend of hers, Wendy, came to New York to see a Beyoncé concert. When I met Wendy, I was appalled that she'd gotten on a plane and travelled from Detroit to New York with her hair looking a hot mess. I didn't say a word but the wild, unkempt hair was distressing to me. But these were millennials. Maybe they didn't care about their image.

The day after they arrived, my niece agreed to meet me at Barclay's Center for the concert since her hotel was in a different direction than my house. I arrived at the concert before she did. When she walked into the venue, I couldn't take my eyes off of Wendy and her natural hair.

"What did you do?" I said, staring incredulously at her hair.

"I gave myself a twist out," Misty said, looking every bit like a glamazon.

A twist out? I'd seen the style before but didn't know the proper name for it. Why hadn't she done that before she got on the plane? She looked amazing.

After the concert, we went to dinner where I quizzed her on her look.

"My hair is natural," she said in a sweet, childlike voice. "So it takes a long time to do."

"I really love it. Why does it take so long?"

"You have to condition well, style it, dry it. And you have to keep twisting it, at night and then do the whole thing over again every few days."

Hmm ... my weave was a shake-and-go type deal.

"Auntie Rhonda, I wouldn't recommend it."

Easy for my niece to say. She'd never had a relaxer a day in her life. Her hair was what my sister's hair used to be—thick, voluminous, and long.

"Yeah, I don't have time to wash my hair every few days," I said. What a departure from my way of thinking as a teen, when I couldn't wash my hair enough. Progress.

I stared at Wendy's hair and let the wheels turn in my head.

I found myself in the throes of the Baader-Meinhof Phenomenon. I'd never thought about natural hair until I'd encountered those women, and now I saw natural hair *everywhere*. Was this just a cognitive illusion or was a social revolution taking place before my eyes? Or both? Actors on TV shows, commercials, movies, models in the pages of magazines were all wearing the hair that I so desperately tried to hide as a child. Springy, fine coils and coarse, tightly drawn curls were all being represented as part of the African American experience. All being represented as beautiful. Oh sure, we all remember Florida from *Good Times* rocking her natural 'do,' but she was an exception. Now, natural African American hair was prolific. At the time of this writing, women rocking natural hair include Lupita N'yongo, Kerry Washington, Viola Davis, Yvette Nicole Brown, Janelle Monae, Solange Knowles, and too many more to count. It was inspiring to see an evolution in hair whereby women embraced their natural locks and still exuded beauty, sophistication and confidence.

But still. I bucked the trend.

38

The fact is, women don't like to talk about money, let alone
deal with it.

Alexa Von Tobel

A Woman's Worth

There was no denying my adoration of Lily. Sitting in her
chair was like sitting in a girlfriend's kitchen while she
baked chocolate chip cookies just for you. Except instead
of baking cookies, Lily styled my hair. She and Collette
had moved to a new shop where they each occupied their
own small, private room. Being in that small room with
Lily catered to my private nature. I could talk to Lily about

anything and not feel as though others were eavesdropping, and she too could speak freely to me. Lily was smart about booking appointments so rarely did I bump into her other clients. As good as it was sitting in her chair, there was always an awkward moment at the end when it was time to settle the tab.

"How much?" I'd ask Lily.

She'd become quiet and shift her supplies around while she … what? Contemplated? Calculated? Vented in her head at me for not knowing how much to pay?

Lily's shop didn't have a menu of prices on the wall. It hadn't for as long as I'd been going to her. Never a strict penny pincher with my money, I could never remember if the relaxer was $55 or $65. Was the trim an extra $5 or $10? What about the rinse? What if I got a relaxer, trim and no rinse? Or a relaxer, rinse and no trim? How much?

"I know what her problem is," Marc said to me one day when I told him how much Lily frustrated me when she procrastinated before telling me the price. "I had the same problem, too."

"What? That you're charging too much?"

"When you like what you do, sometimes you don't see it as a business. You don't want to talk about money. When I edited videos for clients, we'd agree on a price. When I was done, I'd send them an invoice. If one of my crappy clients called me on the phone and challenged the price they agreed upon, I'd feel so uncomfortable, I'd lower the price. I almost felt like I shouldn't be charging anyone anything. I didn't have the mind of a businessman. I mean, I *was,* but I sucked at the part when I had to ask for my fee."

He had a point. Lily grew up in Ghana. I imagined her practicing her hair braiding skills on the neighborhood kids whom she loved, then coming to America to get a license to do hair and begin a professional career. It's possible Lily loved hair, loved her customers so much that talking about money seemed vulgar to her. It was clear she was anguished (annoyed?) in some way by even having to address it.

She mumbled something.

"Huh?" I asked.

"Sixty," she said again, her head down, eyes averted.

I couldn't understand why she wouldn't put herself out of her misery by hanging a price list on the wall. Sure, some cases would demand that more money be charged because of a client's hair, but at least the base price would be for the majority of customers who didn't require extra attention.

Lily's reaction to that question made me feel like a john who'd just been serviced by a hooker. I was serviced and sated, and now I had to deal with the dirty financial business that came next that reminded me this wasn't love at all.

But, as a child does with an alcoholic parent, I learned coping mechanisms. Each time I went to her and had a service done, I added it to the notes section of my Smartphone. For a long time, she and I were able to coast along just fine without me having to ask the dreaded question. No awkward question, no long pause, no averting of the eyes. And then, I went and screwed it all up when I fooled around on Youtube and discovered something totally new to me: crochet braids.

Crochet braids were apparently hot back in the eighties and nineties. The person's hair is cornrowed onto the scalp—much like the beginning of the weaving process. Then a latch hook (exactly like the kind your grandma used to use to make those pictures out of short pieces of yarn that hang on the kitchen wall) is used to attach synthetic hair to the cornrowed hair. The end result is that you've got a head of quickly installed and easily removable hair. Very little skill is needed to achieve the look. However, one must know how to cornrow hair. Cornrows sound like a super simple thing, right? I mean, prisoners in jail cornrow their hair all the time. If they can do it, surely, I can too, right? Wrong. I tried it and ended up with huge gaps between each braid. No amount of fake hair would cover up the gaps. It was disastrous. The solution was simple: I needed a convict to braid my hair. Or Lily. I needed a convict or Lily. Lily was closer so off to Lily I went.

"I need a wash, condition, and then cornrows going all the way to the back," I said.

Lily had heard me express vague interest in going natural. Every time I did, she said, "Hmm … I don't think you're going to like it. It's a lot of work. I don't think it's for you."

I was undeterred. Adding crochet braids to my hair would be the first step toward the process of going natural. And it would be gentle on my mane. I didn't want to be one of those women who became dependent on hair braiders and then started losing my edges because of the tight braids. It was important also that I started learning how to do hairstyles myself. I'd tried the crochet braids before and came out looking like a goofball with bald spots all over my head because my cornrows were too far apart. Solution: let *her* cornrow my hair, and I'd just put the crochet braids in myself.

Here, you might be thinking, why not let her do the whole damned thing? Yes, well … here's a snippet of how that conversation went.

"Lily, have you heard of crochet braids?"

"Of course, I know how to do them. They used to be popular years ago. Now they're making a resurgence."

"I want them. They'll allow me to transition into going all natural."

"They'll look nice on you."

"Can you do them for me?"

"Um hmm," she said.

"How much do you charge?"

A beat. Another beat. And yet another long moment and then, "I'm not sure, I'd have to think about it.…"

"I called around. The going price is a hundred fifty."

"Hmm … That sounds about right."

"Is that what you'd charge?" I asked, knowing I wasn't going to pay someone $150 for something that looked easy enough for me to do, posed no risk to my natural hair, and only lasted a few weeks.

However, none of that mattered because all I got out of Lily was, "Um … I'm not sure.…"

Since I could not do the cornrows myself, and Lily was noncommittal on her price to do the entire crochet braid install, I decided on a solution. My solution was to have her do part of the work that I couldn't do (the cornrows), and then I'd do the rest. And that plan, turned out beautifully. Lily charged me only twenty bucks to wash, condition, and cornrow my hair.

At home, I installed my Senegalese twist crochet braids and they turned out perfect. They were fourteen inches of pre-twisted hair. Traditional braiding would have cost me $150 dollars and eight hours of my time. Crochet braids were a bargain basement priced, DIY braid look that took a fraction of the time and money. It would seem I had a brilliant plan.

Text from me to Lily:

Lily, I have to go to a writer's conference. I need to be out of the shop by noon. Can you do an entire crochet braid? If so, how much will it be? If you don't have time, just braid me, and I can do the rest myself at home. Have to be gone by noon. Let me know.

Response from Lily:

I can see you Saturday at 9.

I was confused. I hate being confused. I had no idea how my Saturday was going to shape up, but I was at the shop at 9 a.m. sharp, as is my nature. It started as it always does: a hug, a kiss, a catch up on family drama. Within an hour I was washed, conditioned, dried, and being braided.

"I brought the hair just in case you have time to install it."

"I don't think I do. I have another client coming soon."

Twenty bucks for cornrows like last time? Cool. It would've been great if she'd confirmed that before I came, but no problem. As long as I was out by noon, I'd still be running on time. When the cornrows were done, she consulted her clock.

"My next appointment isn't here yet. She's been texting me and saying she's here, she's there. She's everywhere but here."

"Hmm," I said, barely registering her comments. The upcoming conference was heavy on my mind.

"This girl is so late. I think I have time to install the braids. You have the hair?"

"Yeah," I said, surprised at this turn of events. I'd been prepared to do that portion of my hair myself. "It's in the car."

"Go get it," she said.

"Sure," I said, figuring it would save me time if she knocked it out herself.

But how much was it going to be? I had budgeted for twenty dollars. All my other money was for my trip.

I went to the car and returned with the hair and the new crochet hook I'd purchased at the beauty supply store. Lily inspected it like a kid with a new toy, smiling the entire time. "This is going to be fun," she said.

Lord, I prayed, *please make it fun and quick.*

When she was halfway done, I looked at the clock. 11:30.

Would I be done by noon?

"What's the matter?" she asked.

"I have to be gone by noon."

"Why?"

"I'm going to a writers' conference this afternoon."

Irritation flashed across Lily's face. She pursed her lips. "I don't like to be rushed," she snapped.

Rushed? Rushed? Did she just say that? Didn't I text her a week ago regarding my time?

I bit my bottom lip as is my pacifist nature and said nothing.

So what if you're a little late, Rhonda? You're not the keynote speaker for heaven's sake. You're just a little ol' attendee. Why is it so important to be on time?

Did I mention I used to get the Perfect Attendance award in elementary and junior high school? Hey, you have your crowning achievements, and I have mine, okay?

I fumed as I watched Lily work. She was a perfectionist. Every braid had to sit just so. Every wisp of hair had to have its place. Which is cool. Except when you're on a time crunch. My leg bounced (aggressive me), and I began to hum (passive me) as I fought to cool my rising temper.

At noon, Lily smiled and said, "Finished. What do you think?"

"It looks great!" I said, anxious to get the dreaded upcoming task done so I could be gone. "How much?"

Silence.

I was growing impatient. Besides the fact that I hadn't budgeted for more than $20 plus tip, I was now officially behind time.

Finally, she said. "One twenty."

I almost hit the roof. No amount of my nice-girl attitude could hide the fact that I was pissed off—with a capital P.

I fished in my pocket for the bills and placed a hundred and forty dollars on the table.

"Thank you," I said between tight lips.

I got into my car and tried to cool my fury. Why couldn't she have told me via text how much she was going to charge so that I could have been financially and mentally prepared for it? I didn't mind spending the money on my hair. I regularly spent $200 for hair weaves alone. Why was she so afraid of the subject of money?

Damn it! I'd forgotten my crochet braid hook. I made a U-turn and dialed her number to let her know I was coming back for the hook. Yes. A $1 hook. I was returning for a $1 hook. It was the principle of the thing.

When I pulled up, Lily rushed out of the shop, her face awash in turmoil. She gave me a warm motherly hug, and, apparently flushed with guilt, pressed the hook and a $20 bill into my palm.

"You okay, sweetie?"

"I'm fine, thanks!" I said with a forced smile on my face. In this moment, I knew I was my father's child. I was pissed but worked hard to reflect calm. I'm certain I failed. I've always struggled to project a nice-girl image. Maybe it was because as a teen, guys catcalling at me would ask me why I looked so mean? I wasn't mean. I went out of my way to prove I wasn't an angry black woman, even when I was very much an angry black woman. By contrast, my mother would have cussed Lily out, told her she shouldn't have waited until after she was done to drop that particular little bombshell, walked out of the shop, and not have given a second thought what Lily or anyone else thought about it.

But I am not my mother. And Lily was too good of a woman to be so easily dismissed. I only wished she knew that her talent was worth all that she charged and then some.

39

In the end, everything is a gag.

Charlie Chaplin

Pretty

I spent much of 2014 on the New Jersey Turnpike. My father had esophageal cancer. I'd drive ninety minutes as often as I could from Staten Island to New Jersey to visit with him. Over the course of a year, it was surreal to see my giant of a father lose so much weight that his body became a bony structure from which skin sagged. I saw so much of myself in him it was eerie. As a child, his coworkers or friends would look from me to him and say, "Jerry, you couldn't deny her if you wanted to."

I didn't get the resemblance so much as a kid. But now I couldn't see anything but myself in his face. The eyes, the brows, even our fingers looked cut from the same blueprint. So much of my features came from him, and it took him lying in a hospital bed to notice the resemblance.

Each trip was different. Sometimes he looked strong and healthy, sitting in his street clothes on the sofa while fussing at his wife about the meals he had or had not eaten and why. Other times, he lay in a hospital bed, barely able to talk. He spoke as if his mouth were weighted with cotton. Dried sleep dotted his eyes. He'd ask me the same questions over and over. He needed a nurse to clean him, change his bedpan. The man who I remembered racing to the end of the fence when I was a child, the man who so graciously let me win, the man who dreamed of being a novelist and an actor but fell short of his dreams, lay in bed, still encouraging me in mine.

His hair turned gray as ash. I touched it, surprised at its softness. Why had I never noticed how cottony soft his hair was? It made me think of my mother's hair, its Native American and Negro blend that was so different from mine. My hair, it would seem, was unlike either of theirs.

It had been months since I last saw Lily. I'd abandoned my quest to go all natural until I felt certain I could maintain the new style and not walk around the world looking like an unkempt ragamuffin. For the time being, I'd found a Dominican hair salon conveniently located near my office. I started going there and felt a certain amount of solace in being able to sit quietly for ninety minutes while I got my hair done. The woman who did my hair didn't speak a lick of English. But she was attentive and efficient, and I always left the shops with relaxed, bone-straight, shiny hair that bounced to the heavens as I walked.

I remembered Lily saying, "These girls go to the Dominican shops because they're cheap. They like to get their hair blow-dried, but our hair wasn't meant for that kind of heat. They always come back to me when their hair is broken and want me to fix it."

I'd go back too, I was sure. I wasn't ready yet. There were phases in taking a break from your stylist. There's the:

1) "I'm taking a break but you know I'll be back because I love you" phase.

2) "Clearly, there's an issue between us" phase.

3) "I've been gone so long how can I even get the courage to ask for an appointment?" phase.

4) "I've waited so long I can never go back" phase.

At that point I was in stage two hovering towards stage three. I never considered for a moment not going back. I was over forty and knew that true friendships were important. People couldn't be dismissed from my life as easily as they were when I was in my twenties. I needed to get over my own issues, get over her issues with money, and move on.

I sat next to my father as he lay on a hospital bed that had been placed in the living room of his home. He was less than a month away from dying, but I didn't know that at the time. I knew he was bad off. He lay staring at the ceiling, then at the walls, drifting in and out of coherence. I wondered what my father—a man who had always had many facts about black history and American and African literature on the tip of his tongue—was thinking about.

"Don't you want to read a book?" I asked.

Being an avid reader, I couldn't imagine the torture I'd feel laying on my back with nothing but my thoughts. I'd go mad.

He lifted his head and looked at me as if I'd asked him if he'd like a Russian child bride for Christmas. He lay his head back down and continued to stare at the ceiling. Off to my left was the television. The news was about to come on.

"You are so pretty."

I turned to my father, stunned.

"What?"

"You are," he said, looking at me with wide eyes as though he'd never really seen me before. "You are so pretty. Do you know that?"

"You're my father. You're supposed to say that."

"No, you are very pretty."

Take a compliment, Rhonda.

"Thank you." I said, feeling immense pride in the compliment.

We both turned to the direction of the television set. A reporter was finishing up a story.

From beside me, I heard my father say, "She is so pretty."

I felt my ego begin to deflate like a balloon losing helium.

And then, the camera focused on the news anchor. I looked at my father. He gazed at her with the same fascination he'd given me only seconds ago.

"She is so pretty. Isn't she? She is so pretty."

As the world began to fade for my father, mine was surrounded by beauty.

And I was part of that beauty.

40

You don't choose your family. They are God's gift to you,
as you are to them.
Desmond Tutu

Family Reunion

Whoever said you can't go home again was right. Nothing
would ever be quite the way the memory recalled it. I
journeyed home for Christmas or Thanksgiving every other
year or so with that in mind. We'd gather at Toya's place
and mill around the apartment as last-minute preparations
were made to the food. There was a time when I used to be
the attention-seeker of the family, always in the middle of

the room telling a joke or story. That year, I sat on the sofa, Marc beside me and watched how much our family had blossomed from our humble beginnings of five females and my nephew all crammed together in our mint green house.

Ma was long retired and in poor health. She owned her home outright—an achievement she loved reminding us about. Like a child let loose in a toy store, Ma bought things, things, and even more things for recreation. Books, CDs, magazines, yarn, bric-a-brac. Everything that had been out of her reach when she was a single mother supporting three kids, a grandchild, and a mother was now available to her. She clogged her home from floor to ceiling with items she swore she needed. There were all kinds of ways to handle loneliness: food, alcohol, sex. Ma bought things. But she no longer had three kids at home to clean for her. A homecoming at her place would have been uncomfortable, if not impossible. Despite her health woes, she looked peaceful on the sofa as she regaled us with stories about the former nursing home patients she encountered in her twenty-year nursing career.

Nina, recently retired from a twenty-year career working customer service for the City of Detroit, looked like she could use another drink. By my guess, she'd already had a few before she'd walked through the door. "I need something to calm my nerves when I deal with Ma," she explained when Ma wasn't around. Nina and Ma had a cordial, yet fractured relationship. I imagined Nina would just as soon visit Ma once a year herself, but she was stuck in Michigan and was perpetually short on cash. They had a dysfunctional codependent relationship, the intricacies of which only they were privy to. But Ma was a healthier enabler than Tony had been. Nina had married him slowly and divorced him quickly. He was twenty years in the wind. Their son, a firefighter, sat on the sofa with his wife and daughter, cracking everyone up about how utterly difficult his firefighter training had been. Boy, the military seemed like a cakewalk in comparison.

But even the military had shifted and morphed into an unrecognizable entity since I'd served. Tamika, Toya's younger of two daughters, caught us up on her three-year enlistment in the Air Force. She was currently stationed in Georgia, and as she spoke I wondered if I had I ever been that young? I watched as she rested her elbows on a table and fiddled with her hair. She was busily snapping the clip of her hair extensions open and closed. (And I thought it was all her own hair.) Tamika's hair was unrelaxed, long and soft as a flower petal. As a child, I would have envied it. Why wear hair extensions when you already have great hair? No, I got it. More is more. The idea of pretending all of that was hers had never even occurred to Tamika. Millennial's were willfully transparent. Tamika continued to play with her extensions.

If there was anyone in our family who'd hit the hair lottery, it was Nikki, Toya's older girl visiting from Tennessee, where she'd moved for nursing opportunities. Nikki's hair was exactly like her mother's had been before Toya had begun applying chemical processes. Nikki's long, thick, wild mane—reminiscent of Diana Ross's hairdo back in the eighties— was that of infinite glory. Or so I'd thought. Nikki, it turned out, was as gifted with hair as Ada and Lily. Toya had been inept with hair and had found herself with two daughters each with an unbridled mass of hair. Nikki learned quickly how to style hair and maintained hers as well as Tamika's. There was nothing she couldn't do: cornrows, box braids, weaves, hell, the girl made her own wigs from scratch. Despite her hair acumen, Nikki could take hair or leave it. If she felt like cutting it, she cut it. If she felt like pinning up her twelve-inches of hair to plop on a homemade one-inch pixie cut wig, she did it. Hair was an accessory, a toy, a tool, not a foundation of purpose or identity.

"Girl, how'd you like him?" Toya asked me late that night when the crowd had dispersed and it was just she and I sitting around a table catching up. Her latest flame had swung by just to say hello. I hope he got a tricycle for Christmas.

"He's cute," I assured her. Toya loved herself some pretty boys: Prince personified. They weren't my cup of Chai, but I couldn't deny his attractiveness. Toya's ex-husband had also been her high school sweetheart. They lasted in their marriage long enough to get the girls raised and then decided that marriage was best left to others. They divorced, and he headed for Texas. Toya was rebounding nicely.

"Now can you tell he's twenty years younger than me?"

Toya should've been ashamed of herself. Toya *was* ashamed of herself. The thing was: she didn't let shame stop her from doing what she wanted to do. While she might've been dangerously close to menopause, her skin was as unblemished as it was when she was thirty years younger. Her figure was rounder, but curves had become all the rage.

"Yes, I can tell he's that much younger than you, Toya. I was gonna offer him some Gerber baby food, but he looked like he'd just eaten dessert."

That amused her to no end. She clapped her hands together and giggled with delicious mischief.

"The first time he slept over...."

"Do I have to hear this?"

"Girl, I kept my wig on," she continued undeterred.

"You went to bed with a wig on?"

Toya giggled like the fifteen-year-old Lolita I remembered her to be. "I didn't want him to see my real hair. When we met I was wearing this wig—which, by the way, I love—and I thought 'How long am I supposed to keep this ruse up?'"

"I think it's safe to say you can take off your wig around the same time you take off your bra. Please tell me you're not still sleeping in a wig?"

"No," she said. "He told me to take it off, and I almost fainted. I was like: you knew all this time? Anyway, he said he liked my real hair better."

"He'd damn well better say that."

"He's really hot, isn't he?"

Remember when I said you couldn't go home? Lots of things change, but sometimes, lots of things stay exactly the same.

41

When I discover who I am, I'll be free.

Ralph Ellison

Home

"Rhonda!" Lily opened the front door of the shop and greeted me with a warmth I did not expect nor deserve. "I've missed you sweetie! What's it been, two years?"

"No!" I said, returning her embrace. Lily was an amazing hugger, and I could have stayed enveloped in her welcoming arms forever. Her accent was music to my ears. "It's only been a year."

I didn't explain *why* it had been a year, and mercifully, she didn't ask.

"Come on back. Tell me what's been going on."

It was like we hadn't missed a beat. I melted beneath her hands as her fingers swept through my hair once again. We caught up on old times and old gossip. After a while the subject came back around to hair, and I reiterated that I was contemplating going natural.

Something about touching my father's hair affected me. I wanted to see if my own hair would feel like his. I hadn't felt my own natural hair since I was a child. But it was more than that. I was tired. For the past year, I'd worn the exact same relaxed straight, plain-Jane, corporate hairstyle, and you know what? I liked the consistency. I was sick of having hair ADD. And because the stylist didn't speak any English, there was never any pressure to change my hair to move with the trends. I wanted to continue along this path, but I also wanted to stop using the burning chemicals on my head that left me with scabs.

"I've been researching the process and the quickest way is to do the big chop."

"Don't cut off all your hair," Lily advised. Lily hated cutting off hair unless it was absolutely necessary. "Where have you been going to get your hair done?"

"A little Dominican place by my job," I said by way of explanation for my absence. "It's so easy to swing by there after work and get my hair done. But then it starts to break off."

"It always does," Lily said, smoothing the cool relaxer on my roots. "If I've said it once, I've said it a thousand times, their drying method is no good for our hair."

"I know, but I loved that bounce."

She laughed. "I know it can become addictive. Until you're bald." She worked on my hair, her full lips curved into a smile. "I got a Christmas gift from you. Every year, no matter what, you always give me a gift. Thank you so much."

"You're welcome," I said, rising from the chair and heading to the washbowl. "Have you noticed my hair has thinned?"

"It happens with age."

"You don't think it has to do with the relaxers?" I said. My thinning hair was yet another reason I wanted to stop with the chemicals. The texture of my hair had completely changed from that of my childhood, just like my sister's. If I continued along the route I was on, I too would need to get rejuvenating shots to thicken my hair.

I was getting sensitive to my thinning hair. Marc, oblivious to the sensitive topic of hair, did a double-take at my scalp one day as I lay on the sofa.

"Hmm," he said nonchalantly when he realized what he was looking at was my scalp. "You've got a bald spot."

I did not have a bald spot, per se. What did he know? What I had was a brand new relaxer that thins out the hair. Once the new growth comes in, voila, no more visible scalp.

But I knew he was on to something. My locks were fine and flimsy, unlike what they were a decade ago.

"Some thinning of hair is caused by relaxing, yes, but I have clients who relax their whole lives, and their hair is nice and thick. With age, our hair thins. Bottom line. You're not a spring chicken any more, Miss Eason."

She smiled down at me with her wide, gapped-tooth grin as my head craned back into the washbowl.

No, I was not a young woman anymore. And I no longer had the energy or desire to chase every hairstyle invented in hopes it would make me feel fabulous on the inside. I was content with myself. Unbelievably, I could look at a woman with a great haircut and not wish it for myself. I had evolved enough to appreciate another woman's style without wanting to trademark it for myself. I no longer experienced jittery excitement when I saw a hairstyle that might look good on me. The anxiousness I felt in buying the right hair, getting the right cut, capturing the exact style that I'd seen was gone. I didn't want change anymore. I wanted peace. I craved consistency.

I didn't want to feel like an indecisive, insecure woman who couldn't figure out what worked for her anymore. And I wanted to feel my hair, just as I felt my father's. Just as I felt my mother's. The hair I ran from as a child was the hair I was ready to run back to. No relaxers. No chemical processes. To date, that relaxer was the last relaxer that Lily would put on my hair.

I'm making no declarations about the future of my mane. Maybe I'll go back to relaxers, maybe I'll throw in a weave, maybe I'll chop it all off and rock a 'fro. I don't know. I've yet to throw away my overflowing Hefty bag of wigs (some with tags still attached) and used weave pieces and new weave pieces. One never knows when a girl might accidentally color her head red on a Tuesday evening and need a quick weave to get her through the week.

What I do know is that the chase has ended. That butterfly can keep right on flitting about. I'm no longer trying to capture it. I'm tired now. I'm 'bout to sit my little ass down somewhere and revel in my contentedness, my hard-won inner peace. For the first time in my life I feel that I'm all right.

Just as I am.

Epilogue

When I discover who I am, I'll be free.

Ralph Ellison

(This quote is a conscious repetition.)

In June 2016, a month after I'd written the end of this book, I had had enough. I was nine months into my transition to all-natural hair. That period sans relaxer had resulted in a thicket of natural coils that was an uncontrollable, embarrassing mess. I needed help fast! I contacted Lily who could not fit me into her schedule. No, I could not wait until next weekend. I needed the creamy crack (also known as a relaxer) on my hair—now.

I found a salon in Jersey that could fit me in. I sat in the stylist's chair resolute in my decision—natural wasn't for me. I needed to feel my fingers glide through silk strands once more. I needed hair that made me look *polished*.

The stylist was Dominican and spoke very little English. Even so, body language is universal. When she had flat-ironed the last piece of my hair, she stood back, threw up her shoulder and hands as if to say, "Eh, it was the best I could do with what I had to work with."

Her standards must have been very exacting because I thought I looked fantastic. I left the salon pleased that the old Rhonda was back. I sat in my car on that hot summer day and admired myself in the mirror. Okay, so my hair was super short. Big deal. At least it was pretty!

And then I got home and really studied my hair. I took a hand mirror and focused it on the top of my head.

Dear God.

No, it wasn't what it looked like.

It couldn't be.

But it was.

A bald spot. I had a bald spot the size of a quarter on top of my head. It was not a trick of the eye. It was not an overactive imagination. I was looking at skin that—upon closer inspection—was shaped like a starfish. I'd wanted a polished look but a gleaming scalp was not what I had in mind.

Holy hell.

I was angry with myself when I recognized that I'd behaved like a drug addict. I'd tried to stop with all of my hair shenanigans and go cold turkey. I was going to love me "just as I am," but then I didn't. Once again, I had fallen into the same dark place I'd been before. Strange salon. Unknown stylist. Harmful chemicals. A whole new me. I'd done all of this before. Hadn't I learned anything? Why do something stupid again if I know where it leads? Because the high is oh so very high. And so I chased it once more.

But this time, the addict OD'd. Now it was time to call in a professional. The dermatologist (a young beauty with raven hair that reached to her backside because God loves His jokes with a touch of irony) ran blood tests and examined a biopsy of my scalp tissue only to tell me what I already knew: I had abused myself. The doctor referred to my condition by its technical name: Central Centrifugal Cicatricial Alopecia, but it was really just self-harm. I had abused myself to the point of hurting the one thing I thought I cared about. My future would be filled with painful steroid injections into my scalp and vitamins and special hair care and a lot more visits.

And as much as I'd like to say that I am a recovered hair-oholic, whole, healthy and happy, I feel that would be a lie.

I am a hair addict in recovery who still loves a fantastic head of hair. I resolve to be kind and gentle to my own in the future, but if I fall off the wagon, I will find a way to climb back on, and love myself in spite of my transgression.

I must learn how to redefine "a friggin' fantastic head of hair" while loving my own. I have to learn how to fall in love with my kinky coils and, by extension, myself.

Of that, I am worthy.

ACKNOWLEDGMENTS

Thank you to Etinosa Agbonlahor who provided me with developmental editing. Your praise of my first draft and editorial direction helped me sort through my thoughts and put them on paper in a way that others would understand and hopefully enjoy. I hope we get the chance to work together again.

Lynn Bosworth is the keeper of one of my huge secrets. I'll tell you that secret if you promise never to tell a soul. Here goes: I don't always know where to put the comma, or the hypen, or the triple or quadruple ellipsis. As my line editor, Lynn helped me chisel this ragged rock into a gem I could be proud to share with others. So glad I found you on

Upwork.com. (By the way, she didn't edit this page so don't hold any errors against her.)

Here's a special shout out to literary agent Miriam Goderich for treating me with kid gloves in our correspondence. Your graciousness didn't go unnoticed.

Last, but not least, my very first agent was Jane Dystel of Dystel, Goderich and Bourret. She worked tirelessly to get this personal narrative in front of major publishers. And she did. Alas, the publishers had little confidence this work could find a market. And they might be right. But a writer's gotta write. And a girl's gotta try. If I've learned nothing else over the years, I have learned how to accept disappointment and get on with it already. So I published this manuscript on my own. Nevertheless, I'm grateful that Jane picked my story out of her slush pile and put in the time and effort to try to get it to the masses.

I'll always be thankful for her belief in my work.

* * * *

If you enjoyed this work, please review from your online retailer so that others may discover and enjoy. Thank you.

357

Made in the USA
Middletown, DE
19 March 2018